The Front National in France

Daniel Stockemer

The Front National in France

Continuity and Change Under
Jean-Marie Le Pen and Marine Le Pen

Daniel Stockemer
School of Political Studies
University of Ottawa
Ottawa, Ontario
Canada

ISBN 978-3-319-49639-9   ISBN 978-3-319-49640-5 (eBook)
DOI 10.1007/978-3-319-49640-5

Library of Congress Control Number: 2016961215

© Springer International Publishing AG 2017
This work is subject to copyright. All rights are reserved by the Publisher, whether the whole or part of the material is concerned, specifically the rights of translation, reprinting, reuse of illustrations, recitation, broadcasting, reproduction on microfilms or in any other physical way, and transmission or information storage and retrieval, electronic adaptation, computer software, or by similar or dissimilar methodology now known or hereafter developed.
The use of general descriptive names, registered names, trademarks, service marks, etc. in this publication does not imply, even in the absence of a specific statement, that such names are exempt from the relevant protective laws and regulations and therefore free for general use.
The publisher, the authors and the editors are safe to assume that the advice and information in this book are believed to be true and accurate at the date of publication. Neither the publisher nor the authors or the editors give a warranty, express or implied, with respect to the material contained herein or for any errors or omissions that may have been made. The publisher remains neutral with regard to jurisdictional claims in published maps and institutional affiliations.

Printed on acid-free paper

This Springer imprint is published by Springer Nature
The registered company is Springer International Publishing AG
The registered company address is: Gewerbestrasse 11, 6330 Cham, Switzerland

Contents

1 Introduction 1
2 The History of the *Front National* 7
   2.1 The Extreme Right in France, 1945–1972 7
   2.2 The Foundation of the FN 10
   2.3 Years of Marginality 12
   2.4 From the Fringes to Party Politics 13
   2.5 The FN in the 1980s and the 1990s 16
   2.6 Crisis and Renewed Success 21
   2.7 The FN Under Marine Le Pen 24
3 The FN's Ideology Under Jean-Marie Le Pen and Marine Le Pen ... 27
   3.1 The FN's Ideology Under Jean-Marie Le Pen 28
      3.1.1 Immigration 28
      3.1.2 Other Features of the FN Programme 31
   3.2 The FN's Ideology Under Marine Le Pen 32
      3.2.1 The FN Ideology in Its Press Releases 35
      3.2.2 The FN Ideology by Regional FN Chapters and the FNJ .. 37
      3.2.3 Quo Vadis Dédiabolisation? 38
      3.2.4 The FN in 2015: Radical Right with a Softened Image .. 40
4 The FN's Leadership and Elites Under Jean-Marie Le Pen and Marine Le Pen 43
   4.1 Leadership: Jean-Marie Le Pen Versus Marine Le Pen 44
      4.1.1 Jean-Marie Le Pen 44
      4.1.2 Marine Le Pen 46
   4.2 The Party Elites Under Jean-Marie Le Pen and Marine Le Pen . 48
      4.2.1 Jean-Marie Le Pen 48
      4.2.2 Marine Le Pen 50

4.3	The FN's Relationship with the Media Under Jean-Marie Le Pen and Marine Le Pen...........................	52
	4.3.1 Jean-Marie Le Pen............................	52
	4.3.2 Marine Le Pen...............................	54
4.4	The Leadership Styles of Jean-Marie and of Marine Le Pen: A Synopsis..	56

5 The FN Membership Under Jean-Marie Le Pen and Marine Le Pen.. 57
    5.1 Method and Interview Sample............................ 58
    5.2 Activists Under Jean-Marie Le Pen and Marine Le Pen......... 62
        5.2.1 Activists' Socio-Economic Background.............. 62
        5.2.2 Activists' Political Socialization.................... 62
    5.3 The Activists' Political Values............................. 67
    5.4 The Activists' Personal Values............................ 71
    5.5 The Activists' Motivations for Engagement.................. 72
    5.6 Engagement Trajectory.................................. 75
    5.7 Changes in Membership Under Marine Le Pen: A Synopsis..... 76

6 The FN Voters Under Jean-Marie Le Pen and Marine Le Pen..... 79
    6.1 Predictors of the FN Electoral Success...................... 80
        6.1.1 Demographics................................. 81
        6.1.2 Socio-economic Factors.......................... 82
        6.1.3 Attitudinal Factors.............................. 84
    6.2 Data.. 85
    6.3 Method.. 86
    6.4 Results.. 86
    6.5 Discussion... 90

7 Conclusion.. 93

Appendix A: The Interviews................................... 99

References.. 101

Index.. 111

About the Author

Daniel Stockemer is Associate Professor in the Department of Political Studies at the University of Ottawa. He specializes in political behavior and political representation. The study of radical right-wing parties in Europe is one of his main research areas. He was awarded an Insight Development Grant from the Social Science and Humanities Research Council of Canada (2013–2016) to study the electoral success of the radical right in Western Europe. He further spent 7 months on fieldwork in France in 2013 interviewing FN members.

His recent work on the radical right in Europe appeared in the *Journal of Common Market Studies, Social Sciences Quarterly,* the *European Journal of Communication*, and *Representation*. He also edited a special issue on the electoral spark of the FN in *French Politics*. Furthermore, he published articles in, among others, *Electoral Studies, Political Studies, European Union Politics*, and the *International Political Science Review*.

Chapter 1
Introduction

On a rainy November morning, dockers from Calais are firing flares in protest against port job losses outside the regional council in Lille, the capital of France's old industrial north. Inside the plush chamber, a tall, solidly built blonde woman in jeans and boots crooks a leg over her knee and flicks through a news magazine. Marine Le Pen, leader of the *Front National*, which has 18 council seats, has dropped in from a day at the European Parliament in nearby Brussels, where the party has 23 MEPs. Le Pen looks bored as the councillors drone on about allocating €1.1 billion of EU money to help revive the bleak economy of Nord-Pas-de-Calais. When her moment comes, she launches into a riff on the evils of the Union. EU funds just reinforce the dictatorship of Brussels and impoverish the downtrodden rural and small-town folk of the region, she says. "I have to remind people ad nauseam that this is not European money. It's part of French taxpayers' money that transits through Brussels with the rest going to pay for central and Eastern Europe." With that, the terror of the French political establishment picks up her papers, closes her beige wool jacket and slips out to a car for the drive back to Paris, missing the council's splendid lunch. So it goes for Le Pen as she tills the fertile electoral soil of the north as the prelude to a run at the Élysée Palace in 2 years' time. (Bremner 2014)

"The *Front National* is at the gates of power" (BBC News 2014). This wake-up call from French Prime Minister Manuel Valls to his dishevelled *Parti Socialiste* (PS) summarizes the attitude of the French political class towards the *Front National* (FN). The mainstream parties, both the PS on the left and the *Union Pour un Mouvement Populaire* (UMP, now called the Republicans) on the right, are frightened: they are frightened that the FN wave continues to sweep over France; they are frightened that the 2002 earthquake, which saw Jean-Marie Le Pen in the second round of the presidential elections, might be repeated; they are frightened that Marine Le Pen could accede to the presidency in 2017. Are these fears justified? Is the FN indeed at the gates of power?

The answer to these questions is not obvious or easy. It is true that the FN has been transformed from a successful yet marginal party to a major player in French politics. Since Marine Le Pen took the reins in 2011, the FN has been successful on three fronts. First, in terms of public opinion, Marine Le Pen has turned the views of a significant portion of the French population in the party's favour. From the 20 to 25 % who perceived the FN as a "party like others" under Jean-Marie Le Pen's leadership, the proportion has increased to over 50 % since Marine Le Pen has been in charge (see, e.g. Le Point 2015). Second, the party has multiplied its membership by a factor of three or four. Whereas the FN had approximately 20,000 members at the turn of the twenty-first century, it had between 60,000 and 80,000 in 2014, making it the third-largest party in France (Stockemer 2014). Finally, the party has reached heretofore unseen electoral heights. In the 2012 presidential election, Marine Le Pen received 18 % of the popular vote. In the 2014 European elections and the 2015 departmental elections, the FN earned 24.9 % and 25.2 % of the votes cast, respectively, ranking it first and second among all French parties in these elections (*Ministère de l'Intérieur* 2015a). The December 2015 regional elections saw a further boost in the FN vote, with 27.9 % in the first round (*Ministère de l'Inté rieur* 2015b). In addition, polls in 2014 and 2015 credited Marine Le Pen with approximately 30 % of voter intentions for 2017, putting her on par with the main centre-right and centre-left contenders (e.g., Alain Juppé and Manuel Valls) or even ahead of them (Le Figaro 2015).

Yet, the FN's successes, particularly in the polls, look somewhat less remarkable if we evaluate them in terms of political representation rather than vote shares. Certainly, 25 % of the popular vote is impressive, but, except in the European and regional elections, this electoral success has not translated into representation. In terms of number of deputies at any level, the FN ranks only sixth in France as of August 2015, making it a rather marginal political force. In addition, it does not, yet, have strong local implementation.[1] Not only does the party still struggle to form local lists, particularly in small and medium-sized towns, but, even more importantly, it did not win any major city in the 2014 local elections. Despite the fact that the FN is in the majority in a dozen municipalities—among others, the party won the towns of Béziers and Fréjus and the seventh *arrondissement* of Marseille—its local power is still marginal; in 2014, it only won 1 in 3000 cities and the majority of the vote in 1 in 1000 municipalities (Shields 2015).

Regardless of how impressive, or not, we might find the FN's electoral and non-electoral victories, it is necessary to put them into perspective: they occurred in a most beneficial structural environment. From 2009 to 2015, France, and Europe, suffered from multiple crises (see Mondon 2014). First is the economic crisis, which started to cripple the country in 2008–2009 and is still lingering, as shown in the unemployment rate of over 10 % and deficits continuously reaching 3 % or more of the state budget. Second, a political crisis is shaking up the political class. Second, President Hollande, discredited by scandal and government inaction, has the lowest approval ratings of any president in the Fifth Republic. The centre right does not score much higher in public approval; following ex-President Sarkozy reclaiming the Republican Party's presidency in 2014, the party is still recovering from internal battles over leadership and programme. With the pending nomination of its presidential candidate in 2016, the party, which is anything but united, is

---

[1]With the regional elections in December 2015, this has probably changed slightly, given the fact that the FN has gained representation in nearly all regions.

likely to face more turmoil. Third, there is a crisis of governance and direction within the European Union. Be it Greece, the refugee crisis, or the North Atlantic Free Trade Agreement, the European Community is facing multiple challenges, and fissures are everywhere between and within European Union member countries.

Given these crises, it is only logical that if the FN should ever be successful, it would in such a beneficial structural environment (McAdam 1988). However, what happens if this structural window of opportunity closes? Can the FN sustain progress in public approval, membership, and electoral results, or will it once again fall back to a position of relative marginality? Answering these questions requires an in-depth analysis of the party, its leader, its programme, its ideology, and its members and supporters. Has the party been transformed after Marine Le Pen was elected to the FN presidency in February 2011? Is it the same party as it was during the 40-year leadership of Jean-Marie Le Pen, or has it evolved into a different party? These are the questions that I seek to answer in this book. More precisely, and using a mixed methods approach, I compare the "old" FN under Jean-Marie Le Pen to the "new" FN under Marine Le Pen across four dimensions: (1) the party's ideology; (2) leadership styles, including the composition of the party elites and the leaders' and party's relationship with the media; (3) the members of the party; and (4) the voters for the party.

In more detail, I evaluate the degree to which there is continuity or change from Jean-Marie Le Pen to Marine Le Pen for these four dimensions, using a supply-and-demand framework (see Klandermans 1986, 1997, 2004). In its original sense, supply refers to the products and services that a company puts on the market, whereas demand refers to the potential buyers of a product in a society, who are susceptible to appeals to purchase the product. In the same way as a company must convince potential buyers of the value and necessity of its products, political parties must convince citizens to rank them favourably, to vote for them, or to join them. Parties can influence citizens in two ways: first, through their programme and ideology; second, through their leadership. A party's ideology, electoral programme, and policy briefs are crucial tools for convincing citizens and supporters to be members and voters of the pertinence and correctness of its positions and of the necessity to fight for its cause.

The book is structured as follows: In Chap. 2, I describe the historical development of the FN, from its modest first steps in politics to becoming a mainstream French party and one of the most successful radical right-wing parties. What ideological changes did the FN undertake after Marine Le Pen took over the presidency from her father in 2011? This is the question that I answer in Chap. 3. Mainly through qualitative textual analysis of FN party documents before and after 2011, which I complement with some quantitative data, I show that there has been very little change in the FN's ideology and programme between Jean-Marie Le Pen and Marine Le Pen. The FN was, and continues to be, the prototypical radical right-wing party. It has always advanced, and still advances, a simplistic frame that pushes anti-immigrant, anti-establishment, and nationalist sentiments. As such, it portrays French society as tainted by foreign influences and governed by corrupt elites that embrace lax government policies in the area of public security (Crépon

2012). The FN embeds these vices in an ethno-centric worldview that puts forward the argument that the nation should be reserved primarily for a certain type of people—those who share the same ethnicity, history, religion, and identity (Hainsworth 2008: 12).

The only major change in Marine's Le Pen's programme is an accelerated turn to the left on economic matters; in the aftermath of her election to the party presidency, the FN has become an essentially nationalistic and socialistic party (see Ivaldi 2015). Using the strategies of populism and anti-elitism (both of which figure more strongly in Marine Le Pen's programme than in Jean-Marie Le Pen's [recent] programmes) Marine Le Pen has tried to appeal to workers and middle-class individuals, the constituencies that arguably suffer the most from economic globalization and the worldwide free-market economic system. Probably even more importantly, there has been a change in the form and rhetoric that the FN uses to communicate its message and advance its positions. Contrary to the old FN, the new FN uses acceptable language, condemns anti-Semitism, and situates its statements within a republican discourse. This change is particularly visible at the leadership level.

Since the supply for action or the success of a party is not restricted to party programmes but also depends on the leaders and their capacity to portray the party's message and to convince citizens, Chap. 4 is dedicated to Jean-Marie Le Pen and Marine Le Pen—their leadership styles, the party elites around them, and their relations with the media. Analysing mainly the secondary literature, as well as some primary sources, I again find more continuity than change in the way the two presidents have run the FN. Both are charismatic leaders who have created a personality cult around their name and governed the FN with an iron fist. The inner party leadership has always consisted of family members and the leaders' faithful followers. Individuals who have posed a danger to the leaders' absolute power or have not followed the official party line have been expelled. However, unlike her father, and in line with the party's rhetorical reorientation, Marine Le Pen has portrayed herself as a moderate leader who not only uses acceptable language but tries to build inclusive electoral lists and solicits professional staff (such as Florian Philippot) to run and professionalize the party.

In fact, these strategies resemble Jean-Marie Le Pen's in the 1980s, when he tried to build a more mainstream and acceptable FN. However, he abandoned this idea in the 1990s. In addition to the differences in rhetoric between the two leaders, the most important difference between Jean-Marie Le Pen and Marine Le Pen is their relationship with the media. Despite the fact that it was in part thanks to the media that the FN became a mainstream political party in the 1990s, Jean-Marie Le Pen always had a strained relationship with them, to say the least. He always perceived his party as a victim of anti-FN media propaganda. However, he also nurtured this negative image by using the media for his provocations and anti-Semitic statements. In contrast, Marine Le Pen has normalized her relationship with the media. Seen as a young and dynamic woman, she is even a media favourite and is regularly invited to appear on talk shows, political shows, and newscasts.

These changes, albeit minor, in party programme and leadership style nevertheless seem to resonate with potential supporters, as the party has been able to significantly increase its membership and electoral support base. Using data from semi-structured interviews that I conducted with nearly four dozen FN members in 2013, I show in Chap. 5 that the reformulated and revived FN message is a good draw for potential recruits. Formerly a party of old, traditional right-wing men and of members with a decidedly far right-wing ideology, the FN membership has changed. It no longer exclusively consists of members with a long family tradition of activism and poorly educated individuals who can no longer cope with the problems of modernization. To the contrary, the FN has mobilized and recruited to its ranks individuals of all ages, social classes, and backgrounds. Rather than appealing to a defined group, Marine Le Pen finds followers among workers, the educated, disgruntled members of the moderate right, individuals who have had negative experiences with immigrants, and members of the French society who have become more conservative or right-wing over the years. These groups form a rather close community in the FN. Yet, the FN community is also characterized by members who prefer to keep their involvement secret and still face some societal discrimination. This demonstrates that despite all of Marine Le Pen's efforts to make the FN a party like the others, it is still not 100 % there.

From survey data on the FN vote in 2007 and 2012, I show in Chap. 6 that the party's voter base has not broadened as much as has its membership. Rather, I find that the new FN could tap more successfully into its core pool. The FN's renewed focus on the lower-middle classes has panned out; in 2012, the largest share of the FN vote stemmed from individuals with low education, workers, and individuals who are dissatisfied with how democracy works in France. Beyond these groups, the FN under Marine Le Pen made some inroads among younger voters and strengthened the voter base in the countryside. In spite of these gains, however, the FN electorate is still quite restricted to specific constituencies. This also implies that the FN has not become a catch-all party.

Quo vadis FN? is the question that I try to answer in the conclusion. I posit that the new FN, under Marine Le Pen, has effectively responded to opportunity structures. In particular, the new FN president has succeeded in giving her party a more moderate and less radical image. I argue that it is exactly this change that the party needed to become more popular among recruits and members. However, I also think that seeing the FN as being on the brink of power is premature. Certainly, the party has broadened its membership, has attracted more votes than ever, and has never been as popular among the French population. This does not mean, though, that it is mainstream; a majority of the population remains opposed to its policy positions (its vote share seems to plateau at 25 to 30 % of the voting-age population). Despite an economic and social climate that is most favourable to the FN, the party continues to lack local implementation. Also, and despite a tremendous rise in membership, the voter base has not really diversified beyond the party's core supporters. Most importantly, it is hardly conceivable that an organization that is more run like a family business than a modern party will gain access to the highest elected office (i.e. the French Presidency) in the twenty-first century.

Chapter 2
The History of the *Front National*

2.1 The Extreme Right in France, 1945–1972

Immediately after the Second World War, there was little space or sympathy for radical right-wing ideas in France. Vichy essentially left a revisionist history of collaboration, which confined the French extreme right to the margins of political life (Kling 2012: 57). In particular, the far-right was the target of *diabolization*, or demonization, in an ongoing attempt to discredit it as a result of its ties to fascism and Nazism (Kling 2012: 58). Nevertheless, several mainly international developments allowed radical right-wing ideas to permeate French society, albeit rather modestly, in the 1950s. Most prominent among the groups that emerged was an extreme-right organization called *Jeune Nation*, founded in 1950 by young army officers disenchanted with the Republic's imminent defeat in the Indochina War (1946–1954). The organization was essentially anti-communist, anti-modernist, xenophobic, and in favour of preserving the empire (Milza 1987: 296).

Following in the footsteps of *Jeune Nation*, other extreme-right organizations came to the fore in the 1950s, focused mainly on the question of Algerian independence. Perhaps the most significant was the Poujadist movement and the party called *Union de Défense des Commerçants et Artisans* (UDCA), which peaked in the 1956 French legislative election, when it won 11.5 % of the popular vote (Kitschelt 1995: 92). Under the leadership of Pierre Poujade, UDCA made frequent appeals to the proponents of *Algérie Française*, which opposed decolonization and Algerian independence (cf. Crépon 2012: 32). More broadly, the 7-year war in Algeria (1954–1962) offered a window of opportunity for the far-right to regain some political space in French society by sparking extreme-right-wing sentiment in the late 1950s and early 1960s. In particular, the wave of secret activities conducted by the *Organisation de l'Armée Secrète* (OAS), a dissident paramilitary organization led by officers and former officers, and the repatriation of one million French colonists after Algerian independence contributed to nationalist feelings and anti-Arab sentiments in France (Betz and Immerfall 1998: 11). Jean-Marie Le Pen was prominent among the OAS's members; he entered national politics as the youngest deputy in the National Assembly, winning a seat for the UDCA at the age 28 (Art 2011: 121).

The Poujadist movement was short-lived but quite successful. In the 1956 legislative elections, the UDCA won 51 seats and some 11.5 % of the popular vote. Two years later, with the creation of the French Fifth Republic in 1958–1959 under Charles de Gaulle's presidency, Poujade and his party disappeared from the political spectrum. Hence, the French far-right remained fragmented in the late 1950s and early 1960s; it did not have the unity or the numbers to repeat the UDCA's 1956 electoral success (Rydgren 2004: 18; Crépon 1999: 33). Realizing this weakness, Jean-Marie Le Pen aimed to unify the nationalist forces by creating the *Comité d'initative pour une Candidature Nationale* in 1963 (DeClair 1999: 25). He resolved to create a truly unified national opposition for the presidential elections in 1965. Le Pen's committee coordinated the presidential campaign of Jean-Louis Tixier-Vignancour (1907–1989). A pro-French Algerian and former adjunct secretary of information in the Vichy government, Tixier-Vignancour was firmly linked with far-right causes[2] (Cohen and Péan 2012). As campaign manager, Le Pen played an important role in Tixier-Vignancour's ability to draw other far-right movements into the fold (DeClair 1999: 26). These included the endorsements of a neo-fascist youth movement called *Occident* (created in 1964) and a far-right periodical, *Europe-Action* (DeClair 1999: 29). Nevertheless, Tixier-Vignancour failed to win more than 5.3 % of the vote in 1965 (Art 2011: 122).

In the late 1960s, the French extreme right remained a conglomerate of political *groupusculaires* (small, isolated groups). Former generations of far-right supporters had been mobilized during the height of *Action Française* and, later, the fight for French Algeria. However, this mobilization could not be sustained beyond these single events. Yet, after 1968, the French extreme right gained renewed energy, as a younger generation of right-wing extremists shifted their political focus away from de Gaulle[3] in search of new issues (DeClair 1999: 29). Aiming to give the extreme right a new ideological footing, a wave of writers and philosophers from the *Nouvelle Droite* (New Right) formed the *Groupe de recherche et d'étude pour la civilisation européenne* (GRECE),[4] which, in 1974, gave rise to its offshoot, the Club de l'Horloge. The *Nouvelle Droite* intellectuals were particularly interested in revitalizing the anti-egalitarian doctrine that had been an important characteristic of

---

[2]For instance, he acted as defence attorney for extreme-right figures such as General Raoul Salan and Colonel Jean-Marie Bastien-Thiry (DeClair 1999: 25).

[3]General Charles de Gaulle (1980–1970) assumed the presidency in 1959, at which time he supported French Algeria. He later changed his mind as the military situation deteriorated, creating a rift within rightist political circles. Though the French far-right had been favourable to de Gaulle, his decision to grant Algerian independence irrevocably separated the far-right camp from the Gaullist mainstream (cf. DeClair 1999: 21–23).

[4]GRECE was a far-right intellectual group whose writings and publications espoused nationalist and racialist principals founded in anti-universalism and a "differentialist" paradigm (which called for the preservation of cultural and ethnic particularities).

the French extreme right before the Second World War (Crépon 2012: 33; Declair 1999: 28). GRECE profoundly inspired the ideological positions of the *Front National* (cf. Dézé 2012: 87; Crépon 2012: 42–47).

At the same time, the extreme right was reinvigorated by youth activism. Alongside *Occident*, which remained popular among young supporters of the French extreme right, new groups formed, including the Jeunesses Patriotes et Sociales, founded by Roger Holeindre[5] in 1968, and the Catholic and Pétainist group *L'Oeuvre Française* (Crépon 2012: 33). The enemy of these mainly youth-based groups was the political left, and they often targeted student-led Communist groups in violent street fights. Still, they were no match for leftist organizations due to a continued lack of coherence among them.

In November 1968, the largest extreme right-wing group in terms of manpower, *Occident* disbanded as a result of its official prohibition following violent protests carried out against leftist student organizations (Crépon 2012: 33). Its leaders regrouped to form other far-right organizations, such as the *Groupe Union-Droite* (GUD). In turn, GUD leaders and a number of former *Occident* members went on to found an activist organization called *Ordre Nouveau* (ON) in 1969. Notable among them were Alain Robert[6] and former *Occident* member François Duprat (1940–1978). ON was different from its predecessors in that its intention was to become a large party representing a unified far-rightist alternative (Kitschelt 1995: 94). Its model was the Italian Social Movement[7] (*Movimento Sociale Italiano*, MSI), and it adopted MSI's strategy for a "National Right" (Dézé 2012: 41).[8] Thanks to this move, ON grew in size and attracted the support of other far-right groups, such as *Une Jeune Europe* and *Action Nationaliste*. By the early 1970s, ON had approximately 5000 members (most of them student activists) operating on the far-right fringes of French politics (DeClair 1999: 31).

---

[5]Roger Holeindre is a former combatant in the Indochina war and the OAS, and former youth director of the *Comité Tixier-Vignancour*. He would later become vice-secretary general of the FN's first executive bureau (Dézé 2012: 33).

[6]Alain Robert was the former director of *Occident* and founder of the GUD. He later became secretary general of the *Front National's* first executive bureau (cf. Dézé 2012: 33; DeClair 1999: 30).

[7]MSI was a neo-fascist political party created by supporters of former Italian dictator Benito Mussolini in 1946.

[8]Giving the party a more respectable image by rejecting violent actions, MSI's Secretary General, Giorgio Almirante, attracted wider support from members of established parties (monarchic parties, Christian Democrats, and Liberals). The party received an unprecedented 8.7 % of the vote in the 1972 parliamentary elections.

2.2 The Foundation of the FN

Even though ON was markedly extra-parliamentarian,[9] its members recognized that a moderate image was needed in order for the movement to become more strongly anchored in French society (Lecoeur 2007: 3–33). Pragmatic ON members became increasingly willing to participate in conventional political activities (Perrineau 1996: 29). After seeing that the MSI won more than 5 % of the vote in the 1970 Italian general elections, ON, pushed by its moderate wing, decided to run candidates in the 1970 by-elections. Receiving 3.12 % of the vote in Paris's 12th electoral district, ON members were strongly encouraged to pursue the parliamentary route. In the 1971 municipal elections, ON received 19,529 votes (2.6 %) in Paris and had isolated successes in other parts of France (for instance, 22 % of the vote on the municipality of Calais [DeClair 1999: 36]). These positive results convinced the majority of ON members that it would be beneficial to create a party composed of far-right groups and individuals (DeClair 1999: 36–37).

In June 1971, ON's political programme began to take shape with François Duprat's manifesto, *Pour un Front National* (For a National Front) (Dézé 2012: 38). The manifesto buttressed traditional extreme-right-wing values; it continued the tradition of "the belief in natural order, the defense of certain traditional values, suspicion of democracy (at least in its parliamentary form), xenophobia, and even latent anti-Semitism" (Roussel 1985: 95). Supported by Duprat's programme, the ON rallied the forces of the far-right in hopes of making political gains in the 1973 legislative elections (Crépon 2012: 34) and officially became a party in June 1972, under the name *Front National pour une Unité Française* (FNUF). The name was to be interpreted in a literal sense, providing a political "front" behind which far-right activists could pursue their goals (Williams 2006: 82).

The FNUF, as ON intended, was modelled upon the MSI and even copied the party's emblematic tricolour flame (Williams 2006: 82; Rydgren 2004: 18). The FNUF displayed revolutionary tendencies insofar as it called for a break with the past that would lead to a "French renaissance and a new defence" of the French people (Berezin 2007: 141). However, it did so under the guise of parliamentarism. For this purpose, it needed to create a façade by presenting a leader who could bring electoral credibility to the party (Crépon 2012: 35). By the intermediary of Roger Holeindre and François Brigneau, Jean-Marie Le Pen became the first president of the new party[10] (Art 2011: 123). This choice was based on his prior experience in French politics and his public image as a relatively moderate right-wing politician. On October 5, 1972, the *Front National pour une Unité Française* became the *Front*

---

[9]ON members were partisans of the *Revolution Nationale*, a nationalist movement that called for the demise of the Fifth Republic and the subsequent establishment of an authoritarian regime (Art 2011: 123).

[10]Jean-Marie Le Pen is often credited with creating the *Front National*. In reality, the party was created by several individuals: François Brigneau, François Duprat, Alain Robert, and Jean-Marie Le Pen (Declair 1999: 57).

National (FN) (Berezin 2007: 131; Kitschelt 1995: 94). The heterogeneous organization brought together any number of Poujadists, neo-fascists, anti-Gaullists, activists, and right-wing intellectuals (Betz and Immerfall 1998: 12; Bourseiller 1991: 78–83; Soudais 1996: 184–187).

The party strove to present itself as a populist, xenophobic movement that transcended traditional conceptions of left and right (Davies 1999: 7). The party's goals and ideology were summarized in the FN's original publication, "Defending the French—*The Front National Program*" (1973). In addition to its nationalistic, and at times racist, policy prescription, the FN advocated the shrinking of the public sector, the minimization of state intervention, drastic changes to immigration policy, Anti-Europeanism, and proportional representation (Camus 1996: 20). However, themes such as nationalism, immigration, and security were not high on the public agenda at the time and were thus dismissed as propaganda (Kling 2012: 18).

From the outset, internal conflicts proved to be a serious impediment to the new party's organizational development. The FN failed to formulate a cohesive programme as schisms arose between the extremist nationalists and the more moderate supporters of Le Pen[11] (Kitschelt 1995: 94). This ideological rift was crystallized as a result of the FN's poor performance in its first national election. On March 4, 1973 in the legislative elections, the FN was unable to deliver on expectations, securing only 108,000 votes, or 1.32 %, nationally (Camus 1996: 21).

The FN's poor electoral showing aggravated the thematic rift, and two contradictory courses of action were put forward: ON members sought to withdraw from electoral politics and return to their militant activism, whereas Le Pen advocated strengthening the party (DeClair 1999: 39). This ideological and strategic division was ultimately resolved on June 21, 1973, when ON was banned from politics after a violent clash with the Communist League in Paris. The ban took effect after an ON meeting called *Halte à l'immigration sauvage* (Halt to wild immigration) during which ON members clashed violently with members of the radical left (these clashes included the use of guns). The meeting was finally ended by police intervention (Camus 1996: 21). With the FN missing its backbone, Le Pen and his friends were able to gradually take control of the party (Perrineau 1998: 29–30).

Nevertheless, the secession of ON was costly for the FN in the short run; the party lost a substantial portion of its support base as well as its investments in the electoral campaigns (Dézé 2012: 54, 58–59). In addition, although ON dissolved, its members continued to contest with Le Pen and his party in 1973, taking up the slogan *Faire Front* in direct opposition to the FN (Art 2011: 123). In 1974, a different group of former ON members founded yet another radical right-wing party, the Party of New Forces (*Parti des Forces Nouvelles*, PFN), in order to

---

[11]The revolutionary nationalists remained stanchly antiparliamentarian, whereas supporters of Le Pen generally accepted the republican democratic system (Art 2011: 123). The FN became divided between "pragmatists", who conceded the need for a strategic change in view of ON's politics, and "radicals", who feared the dissolution of the FN's nationalist thrust (cf. Dézé 2012: 45–49).

compete with the FN in parliamentary elections. The FN and the PFN had divergent political strategies, particularly with regard to political alliances. Le Pen categorically refused to negotiate with mainstream right-wing parties, whereas the PFN was favourable to alliances that could defeat the left (Kling 2012: 19). Despite some media attention and the founding of the FN's youth organization, the *Front National de la Jeunesse* (FNJ), in 1974, the renewed division of extremist forces all but crushed the FN's electoral ambitions for nearly a decade (DeClair 1999: 167; Betz and Immerfall 1998: 12).

2.3 Years of Marginality

The far-right remained marginal in the French political landscape during the 1970s (Art 2011: 123; Kitschelt 1995: 94), despite several attempts to break away from its position on the fringes of French society. As part of its attempt to improve voter support, the party modified its ideological stance by abandoning some of its most radical positions (e.g. it stopped accusing outside influences of being responsible for France's decadence) and adopted a more general position against infringements on the country's national identity (Camus 1996: 24). Despite these changes, the FN was unable to obtain more than 0.62 % of the vote in the 1974 presidential election (Perrineau 1996: 30). Realizing the necessity to become more firmly anchored to and connected with other far-right-wing groups, Le Pen developed ties with others on the far-right, including national socialists and Catholic fundamentalists. In 1974, François Duprat and his national revolutionist group were integrated into the FN.[12] Three years later, in 1977, Jean Stirbois and the solidarist movement joined the party.[13] In terms of ideology, the arrival of these two groups did not bring the FN closer to mainstream politics. Instead, the FN continued to embrace an ideology that included racism, militarism, anti-democracy, and virulent anti-communism (Ivaldi 1998).[14]

The influx of these radical right-wing factions did not prove beneficial to the FN in elections. To the contrary, the FN remained marginal in electoral politics, obtaining fewer than 200,000 votes (0.29 %) in the 1978 legislative elections (Perrineau 1996: 30). In the second round of the elections, Le Pen also faced a

---

[12] As a former member of *Jeune Nation* and *Ordre Nouveau*, Duprat was a very influential figure in the French far-right. He also convinced many extreme-right factions to join the FN, including the *Fédération d'Action Nationale et Européenne* (FANE) and the *Groupes Nationalistes Revolutionaires* (GNR). In the mid-1970s, the FN managed to attract approximately 300 GNR and 500 FANE members, bringing its total membership to just under 1000 (Dézé 2012: 60).

[13] The solidarist movement advocated a third way, supporting neither the Soviet Union nor the United States of America (Marcus 1995: 65).

[14] Duprat's national revolutionist movement was characterized by a very aggressive anti-communist stand. Among others, it advocated that force was the only way to deal with communists (see Birenbaum 1992).

dilemma; he was being pushed by the media and some factions within his party to choose between supporting the centre-right party and the left-wing party, or, as he referred to it, to choose between "diarrhea and cancer" (DeClair 1999: 180). When he chose to support the centre-right, there was a certain amount of dissension among the "revolutionary nationalists" (DeClair 1999: 180). The FN suffered an additional blow in 1978. Duprat, who by then had become the second-in-command of the party and Le Pen's chief aide, died in a car bombing. For Le Pen and his party, this resulted in a double loss: first, Le Pen lost his main organizer; second, many of the national socialists who had joined the FN with Duprat in the mid-1970s left the party. As a result, the FN's dismal electoral performance continued in the 1981 presidential elections. Le Pen failed to receive the 500 signatures[15] required to run in the 1981 presidential contest (Kitschelt 1995: 94). Consequently, the FN was powerless to prevent a Socialist victory in the presidential election that year (Kitschelt 1995: 97).

2.4 From the Fringes to Party Politics

Yet, to cite Le Pen, the period of "crossing the desert" did not last forever for the FN (DeClair 1999: 42; Williams 2006: 83). Although detrimental in the short run, over the long run the Duprat incident proved to be an opportunity for the FN to engage in electoral politics by stripping itself of direct associations with Nazi or fascist parties (cf. Camus 1996: 35–36; Hainsworth 2000; Simmons 2003). In particular, it allowed the FN to potentially open its support base towards veterans, professionals, and students (in Betz and Immerfall 1998: 15). These groups became also more attuned to supporting the FN ideology because the social climate began to change in the early 1980s. In fact, the FN's rise in electoral politics was directly linked to social, economic, and political transformations that occurred in France starting in the early 1980s. In particular, three structural factors proved beneficial for the FN.

First, there was some latent unhappiness within the French population about law and order after the Socialists took office in 1981. For example, Mitterrand's decision to use his presidential prerogative to release 6200 prisoners, almost 14 % of France's inmates, in the summer of 1981 (Shields 2007: 200) created uneasiness: the granting of amnesty to so many prisoners was viewed as too generous by 61 % of the respondents to a survey (Favier and Martin-Roland 1990: 179). Other controversial policy reforms in the early 1980s included the revocation of the right of the police to conduct random security checks and two laws that circumscribed police powers. Conservative individuals and proponents of a

---

[15]In France, a candidate's placement on the presidential ballot is contingent upon the solicitation of 500 signatures from mayors, senators, National Assembly deputies, or other official representatives. In the 1981 presidential elections, Le Pen was unable to secure the sponsorship signatures and thus could not run (cf. DeClair 1999: 44).

strong France, among others, thought that these reforms went too far and compromised public security.

Second, the French population became increasingly sensitive to issues related to immigration (Ignazi 2013: 71). Under Mitterrand, immigration regulations and enforcement measures to take illegal immigrants back to the border were eased. The same applied to obstacles to reuniting immigrant families; these, too, were partly removed. Through the emergence of prayer rooms in the workplace and an increase in the number of mosques (the number of mosques surged from under a dozen in 1970 to almost 1000 at the end of the 1980s), religious pluralism became a reality in French cities (Shields 2007: 201)—a development that did not sit well with conservatives and traditional Catholics.

It was not simply the increase in the number of immigrants that was frightening to parts of the French population but also the proportion of North Africans, who by the 1980s had become a very visible minority. In 1946, immigrants from North Africa and the Maghreb represented 2.3 % of the foreign population, whereas 88.7 % were European. In contrast, in 1982, the proportion of European immigrants had decreased to 47.6 %, whereas North Africans represented 38.5 % of all immigrants (Weil 1991: 374–375). Although North Africans had first been temporary migrants who came to fill manual labour jobs, they became a permanent addition to the country under Giscard d'Estaing's presidency (1974–1981). Some people associated immigrant families who moved into social housing with increased ghettoization and higher crime and delinquency rates in those housing projects. Moreover, there were fears that immigrants from Northern Africa would be incapable of adapting to French culture (Shields 2007: 203).

Third, many voters were dissatisfied with the intensity and duration of the economic crisis in the late 1970s and early 1980s (Perrineau 1996: 33). After the two oil shocks (1973 and 1979) and the rise in unemployment under Giscard d'Estaing's government (more than 1.5 million people were jobless), Mitterrand sought to implement a neo-Keynesian economic policy to promote growth and reduce unemployment. The government nationalized several industries and banks, created 150,000 public-sector jobs, offered loans and subsidies to companies, and raised wages and welfare benefits. However, these policies resulted in a government budget deficit. The rise in wages reduced the profits of French companies, resulting in a decrease in investment and job creation. Furthermore, because of the overvalued franc, France's competitiveness on the international market was reduced; as a consequence, French enterprises struggled to export their goods. Finally, the increase in public consumption profited neighbouring countries such as West Germany (Shields 2007: 198). Altogether, the economic policies implemented by Mitterrand resulted in an increase in unemployment, recorded at 1,794,900 people in May 1981 and 2,005,000 people in May 1982 (12 % increase) (Favier and Martin-Roland 1990: 114). The public-sector spending also had negative effects on the government's ability to control inflation (which was as high as 14 % in the early 1980s) (Shields 2007: 200).

In the early 1980s, the FN capitalized on these developments by creating a new image centred on immigration and security (Simmons 2003: 67; Williams 2006: 82).

2.4 From the Fringes to Party Politics

In particular, Stirbois and his supporters became a central component within the party pushing forward reforms.[16] Most important, the FN attempted to hasten the rise of the immigration issue in public awareness. The party made the connection between immigration, on the one hand, and crime and unemployment, on the other hand. In a strategic move, it also capitalized on the socioeconomic crisis to advance xenophobic and authoritarian elements that had already become ingrained in the French political fabric. Similarly, the FN's defence of French nationals politicized anti-establishment attitudes (Arnold 2000: 254).

In another strategic move, Le Pen replaced the party's extremist discourse with a populist message that could appeal to a much wider audience (Marcus 1995: 12; Art 2011: 125). The FN began to use populism both as a means of differentiating itself from mainstream parties and presenting itself as an alternative to the political status quo. In particular, the FN-affiliated think tank GRECE had a significant influence when the party adapted some new language that emphasized concepts such as "difference", "identity", and "exclusion" (Davies 1999: 21). For instance, the FN embraced discourses that proposed exclusionary conceptions of community, thus countering the ideals of an internationalized and multicultural society (e.g. Mayer 2002; Ignazi 2003; Betz 2004). Finally, the FN and its leader effectively denounced the anti-colonial and integrationist values put forward by the left (Frey 1998: 74).

After the leftist win in the 1981 presidential elections, both main centre-right parties, the Union for French Democracy (UDF) and the Rally for the Republic Party (RPR), revised their platforms to adopt a more aggressive discourse and a more radical stance on immigration and social matters in order to reaffirm their conservative positions. In turn, this enabled the FN to gain legitimacy, as these new positions resembled their own (Ignazi 2013: 76–77). In addition, faced with ever-growing unemployment and social problems, such as the ghettoization of the suburbs around large cities such as Lyon and Marseille, many voters were losing faith in the established political system and confidence in its ability to address key issues. This resulted in a high level of pessimism about France's future, a problem on which the FN could capitalize (Ignazi 2013: 73).

The FN's electoral breakthrough came between 1981 and 1983 (Bornschier and Lachat 2009: 365). The party's 1981 legislative election campaign in the small town of Dreux provided its first partial success. Dreux was composed mainly of unskilled labourers living in public housing, who had witnessed a steady influx of immigrants during the 1960s and 1970s[17] (Kitschelt 1995: 100). Le Pen and Stirbois organized support for the FN based on anti-immigration appeals, which they linked to insecurity and unemployment. This position resonated with voters; in Freedman's (2004: 40) view, it was the single most important issue through which

---

[16]Jean-Pierre Stirbois was a former Union solidariste member and activist for *OAS-Metropole*. He was among the most active members of the Tixier-Vignancour movement (Dézé 2012: 69). In 1977, he was appointed to the FN's political bureau, and he quickly became secretary general of the Comité Le Pen and, after 1978, second-in-command of the FN (Dézé 2012: 70).

[17]By the 1980s, the immigrant population in Dreux had reached approximately 30 % (Kitschelt 1995: 100).

the FN mobilized support. In fact, strong grass-roots mobilization and the exploitation of immigration as a main cause for unemployment and insecurity allowed the party to garner 13.6 % of the vote in Grande-Synthe and 12.6 % in Dreux-Ouest (Perrineau 1996: 41).

In the 1983 municipal elections, the FN was able to consolidate these successes. Le Pen won an astounding 11.26 % of the vote in the first round and was appointed municipal councillor in the 20th arrondissement of Paris. As it had in Dreux, Le Pen's campaign proved effective in neighbourhoods where unemployment was high and foreigners were poorly assimilated (DeClair 1999: 60). For his part, Stirbois won 16.72 % of the vote and was elected to the municipal council in Dreux (Charlot 1986: 43). Following these partial electoral victories, Le Pen capitalized on the media attention that he and his party received (see also Chap. 3). For example, he appeared on a television interview programme called *L'heure de vérité* (The Hour of Truth) on February 13, 1984 and embarked on a nationwide promotional tour. These efforts proved fruitful; by the spring 1984, 7 % of the French population indicated that they would vote for the FN, if they had to vote now. In Kling's (2012: 34) view, the FN was beginning to find an echo throughout France.

The momentum generated by the media and the municipal elections led to the FN's first national electoral success in 1984. The European elections that year sent shockwaves through France's political landscape (Betz and Immerfall 1998: 21; DeClair 1999: 61). Although a meagre 57 % of the discontented electorate bothered to cast a ballot, no fewer than two million voters (11.2 %) cast a vote for the FN (Betz and Immerfall 1998: 13). The proportional representation system and societal concerns over unemployment, immigration, security, and cutbacks in social services had played to the FN's strength (Dézé 2012: 75). To the surprise of established parties and the media, the party appeared to have suddenly shifted from the fringes of politics to become a major player in the French partisan system (DeClair 1999: 63).

2.5 The FN in the 1980s and the 1990s

The FN's 1984 electoral success not only increased its political visibility and legitimacy but also enabled it to build an organizational structure which attracted recruits at the grass-roots, mid-rank, and intellectual levels (Rydgren 2004: 19). For example, as part of their effort to professionalize the party, two cadres, Carl Lang and Martial Bild, created a school to train party elites and formed standing committees on various issues (DeClair 1999: 198). In addition, the party instituted an "organizational backbone" of politically experienced activists and

2.5 The FN in the 1980s and the 1990s

candidates[18]—most notably Edouard Frédéric-Dupont and Bruno Mégret[19] (Rydgren 2004: 19).

These strategic changes boded well for the French far-right, as the FN won a national victory in the 1986 legislative elections. The party ascended to the National Assembly under the slogan *Rassemblement National* (National Rally) (Dézé 2012: 83). It garnered a respectable 9.65 % of the vote and won 35 (out of 577 seats)[20] (Pedahzur and Brichta 2002: 42; Kling 2012: 41). Noteworthy is that, in its attempt to limit socialist losses and weaken the moderate right, the Mitterrand government had changed France's electoral system from a two-round majoritarian system to proportional representation, thus allowing FN representation (Betz and Immerfall 1998: 21). In other words, strategic considerations by the French left were partly to blame for the ascendance of the FN and its representation in parliament. French voters were disillusioned by these electoral games and by the inability of established parties to address social concerns ranging from pensions to Islamic fundamentalism.

In such a situation of general dissatisfaction, the FN's populist discourse became well known, as Jean-Marie Le Pen regularly denounced the policies of the "gang of four"[21] and the "system candidates" (Bornschier 2005: 23). The FN's populist strategy appeared to be effective, as its key issues were being increasingly absorbed by mainstream parties (cf. in Boulanger 1990: 37–40). The party brought its concerns to the top of the national political agenda, thereby forcing other political parties to take positions on particular issues—most notably immigration (Davies 1999: 1). Centre-right parties and politicians also borrowed elements of Le Pen's anti-immigration rhetoric as a competitive tactic to advance their own policy agenda[22] (Betz and Immerfall 1998: 22). For instance, former president Giscard d'Estaing lamented the "immigrant invasion" in the *Figaro Magazine* (DeClair 1999: 93). Yet, the mainstream right's attempts to co-opt the immigration issue

---

[18]Other well-known intellectuals and politicians involved included Yvon Briant, Jean-Yves Le Gallou, Pascal Arrighi, and François Bachelot (DeClair 1999: 64).

[19]Bruno Mégret left the RPR (1978–1981) and joined the LePenist movement in 1985. He became highly influential among these new members. In particular, he is known for creating the FN's radical anti-immigration programme (1991), which outlined "50 concrete measures", including cancellation of naturalizations granted after 1974 and repealing the "anti-racist laws" that protect minority rights (Betz and Immerfall 1998: 16).

[20]The FN temporarily made an alliance with the *Centre National des Indépendants et Paysans* (CNIP) party for the 1986 legislative elections.

[21]The FN used the term "gang of four" to describe what the party viewed as a corrupt oligarchy at the centre of French politics: the RPR (*Rassemblement pour la République*), the UDF (*Union pour la Démocratie Français*), the PS (*Parti Socialiste*), and the PCF (*Parti Communiste Français*) (cf. Davies 1999: 4).

[22]For instance, hard-line Gaullists adopted tough anti-immigration rhetoric in the lead-up to the 1988 presidential elections in order to keep Gaullist voters from deserting to the FN (Merkl and Weinberg 1993: 41). However, in making the decision in 1988 to distance itself from the FN, the RPR government played into Le Pen's hands (in Merkl and Weinberg 1993: 41). The anti-immigration policies pursued by the post-1993 conservative government and the RPR interior minister, Charles Pasqua, also attested to the FN's influence in France's mainstream politics (Kitschelt 1995: 119).

redounded to the FN's advantage, giving credibility to the party's ethno-pluralist rhetoric and allowing Le Pen to assert that voters "prefer the original over the copy" (Mudde 2007: 241; Goodliffe 2012: 151; Betz and Immerfall 1998: 22). Likewise, the FN's nationalist standpoint was almost the exact opposite of the Socialists' "cosmopolitan" perspective during the Mitterrand era. This contrast enabled the FN to rail against the notions of integration and multiculturalism endorsed by the PS (cf. Davies 1999: 4).

In this propitious climate for the FN and Jean-Marie Le Pen, the party had its best-ever showing in the 1988 elections. Thanks to a well-planned campaign, under the slogan *"Le Pen, Le Peuple"* (Le Pen, the People), and a strong organizational capacity, the FN won 14.38 % of the vote in the presidential elections (DeClair 1999: 81). Its total vote (4,375,894 votes) represented unprecedented political progress in just 4 years. In absolute terms, the FN doubled its vote share from the 1984 European elections; this success was sufficient to solidify its place in national politics (Crépon 2012: 70). However, its showing at the legislative elections in 1988, which were held simultaneously with the presidential election, was less stellar. Although the party garnered a respectable 9.7 % of the vote, or 2,350,000 votes, the vote of the FN decreased, compared to the legislative election in 1986, in 115 districts. In addition, the return to the two-round majority system deprived it of basically all national representation. Not a single FN candidate received a majority in the first-round vote (Crépon 2012: 83), and only one candidate, Yann Piat, defended his seat, in Var's 3rd district.

More generally, by the late 1980s, the electoral success of the FN had plateaued. The media had become indifferent or hostile to Le Pen's frequent provocations, thereby depriving him of a national audience and significantly reducing his political prospects (Merkl and Weinberg 1993: 42). Le Pen's provocations also shone a negative light on the party. They had started on September 13, 1987, when, during an interview on *Grand Jury RTL-Le Monde*, Le Pen infamously referred to the gas chambers in Nazi Germany that killed millions of Jews as "a detail" in the history of the Second World War (Kling 2012: 68; DeClair 1999: 89). One year later, in another reference to the gas chambers built by the Nazi regime, Le Pen referred to the minister of public service at the time, Michel Durafour, as *Monsieur Durafour Crématoire*.[23]

Already weakened by Le Pen's *gaffes*, the FN faced a difficult challenge, especially in small towns and villages, in the 1988 municipal elections held at the end of that year, which required candidates for 36,000 communes. Lacking sufficient human resources, the party's leadership decided to concentrate its efforts on large urban areas. Even so, only 214 out of the 390 cities with a population of over 20,000 had an FN candidate (Perrineau 1998: 41). Despite some local successes (e.g. the party received 33 % of the vote in Marseille), the party's momentum appeared to have stalled. The crisis was aggravated by Stirbois's death in a car accident in November 1988 and the defection of no fewer than 18 regional

---

[23]To explain the play of words, four (in French) means oven.

councillors to the National Centre of Independents and Peasants (*Centre National des Indépendants et Paysans*, (CNI)), RPR, and UDF (DeClair 1999: 64, 162). Nevertheless, predictions of the demise of the FN were premature.[24]

Despite internal problems, increased criticism by the media, and the tacit agreement of republican parties not to forge an alliance with it, the FN secured 11 % of the national vote in the 1989 European elections (DeClair 1999: 91). It seemed that some internal reshuffles had borne their first fruit. In October 1988, Bruno Mégret was appointed general director of the party. As such he was in charge of the party's discourse and political strategy with the goal of establishing the FN's hegemony over right-wing politics (Perrineau 1998: 41). In particular, Mégret played a vital role in the popularization of the FN's rhetoric. Under his direction, the party changed the style of its programme and reformulated its xenophobic and exclusionary elements into politically normalized expressions[25] (Betz and Immerfall 1998: 17). In doing so, he strengthened the party's strategy of polarizing the political debate about its ideas and reached beyond its core constituency (Betz and Immerfall 1998: 17). Also in 1989, Mégret created the FN's in-house think tank, Conseil Scientifique. This initiative sought to improve the party's image in the academic sphere, in order to remove it from its marginal position within French politics (Gauthier 2009: 388).

After some internal turmoil in the early 1990s (several hundred party members renounced their party allegiance when the FN denounced the US-led foreign intervention in the first Gulf war in 1991 [Maréchal 1994: 45]), the last decade of the twentieth century offered several openings for the FN. In particular, the end of the Cold War and the beginning of the era of globalization, which became an extremely salient issue in French national politics, offered the FN a window of opportunity. Responding to social and economic globalization, the party developed a sophisticated argument against the nature of global capitalism and advocated a form of popular capitalism[26] that placed more emphasis on social and anti-neoliberal economics (Minkenberg and Perrineau 2007; Kitschelt 1995: 91). In this reformulation of its economic policy, which put more stress on the needs of the poor, the FN's guiding principle remained that the economy must serve the interest of the nation (Bornschier 2005: 32). As such, it arguably evolved towards "economic nationalism" characterized by a focus on national preference and protectionism (Davies 1999: 24). This repositioning also allowed it to advocate a "third way" between liberalism and socialism: "Neither Left nor Right: French" (Davies 1999: 22; Rydgren 2004: 128). The result was a market-liberal, anti-state

---

[24]For example, Simone Veil, a cabinet minister for Valéry Giscard d'Estaing and president of the European parliament, stated in December 1989 that the FN had arrived at its final chapter and was on the verge of collapse (Perrineau 1998: 39).

[25]For instance, by presenting a differentialist discourse under the slogan *Les Français d'abord* (The French first), Mégret skirted the anti-racist legislation and advanced a "disguised" xenophobia under an a priori principle of non-exclusion (Dézé 2012: 91).

[26]Other terms for popular capitalism are "political entrepreneurialism" and "capitalist-authoritarianism" (cf. Minkenberg and Perrineau 2007; Kitschelt 1995: 91).

programme with populist-authoritarian aspects (Betz and Immerfall 1998: 14). In addition, the theme of globalization was incorporated into its political strategy and linked to populism, immigration, and security.

During the 1990s, the FN's populist appeal remained popular (Rydgren 2004: 112). The party's self-definition as the alternative to the mainstream moderate parties was being increasingly absorbed by a large portion of its supporters.[27] Moreover, the FN had effectively influenced the mainstream right's discourse on immigration and insecurity. This polarized the rightist camp and shifted attitudes within traditional political cleavages (Lecoeur 2003a, b). For instance, the FN's nationalist discourse had gained considerable ground as rising fears about an impending monetary union led to declining support for the European Union.[28] As a result, the FN modified its divisive "us/them" discourse to include new political "enemies" such as elites from the European Union and international political institutions (Lecoeur 2003a, b). To remain as credible as possible, the party's new populist discourse matched these new considerations with familiar national-populist themes, including immigration and xenophobia; authoritarianism and authoritarian law-and-order policy; and a continued anti-party/system stance (Evans and Ivaldi 2005: 354).

This populist strategy translated into the FN winning up to 15 % of votes cast by the mid-1990s (Arnold 2000: 255). It received 13.9 % of the vote in the 1992 regional elections—more than triple the amount of votes (4.2 %) it received in the 1986 elections (DeClair 1999: 92). It more or less consolidated this proportion in the 1993 legislative elections, boasting 12.4 % of the total vote and 100 candidates passing the 12.5 % threshold in the first round (Rydgren 2004: 20). Le Pen's anti-EU campaign in the 1994 European elections earned the party 10.5 % of the vote and 11 seats in the European Parliament (Kling 2012: 94; DeClair 1999: 97). The year 1995 proved particularly successful for Le Pen and his party. In particular, the FN continued to benefit from Mégret's ability to provide skills and resources during the many elections in that year. As social cleavages rose between supporters of national sovereignty and Europeanization, Mégret formulated an isolationist discourse that framed the FN as a defender of the French nation (Crépon 2012: 49–50).

In the municipal elections held in the spring of 1995, a total of 1075 FN councillors were elected, while only 360 left office (Kling 2012: 87). In addition, the FN elected 250 regional councillors and three mayors in fair-sized cities.[29] Also

---

[27] For instance, a 1990 survey showed that 71 % of FN activists who were delegates to the party's 1984 national convention would have abstained in the second round of any elections if the choice was between a candidate from the moderate right and a socialist (Ysmal 1991: 189–191).

[28] Debate was particularly heated over the ratification of the Maastricht treaty. The narrow margin by which the initiative was ratified by the Socialist/RPR government was a repudiation of Mitterrand and underscored the discontent of French citizens with EU policy-making. Le Pen seized the opportunity to be a leading voice against these policies for EU integration (cf. DeClair 1999: 96). These mainly economic policies provided him with a discursive platform for cultural differentialism.

[29] The FN took political power in Marignane, Toulon, and Orange (Perrineau 1997: 82).

that year, the party peaked in the parliamentary elections by winning 14.9 % of the votes cast (Rydgren 2004: 21). The corruption scandals that surfaced among ruling parties helped revitalize the FN's anti-establishment rhetoric during the 1995 presidential campaign.[30] Le Pen gained 15 % of the vote, with the support of 30 % individuals in low income jobs, 25 % of the unemployed, and 18 % of workers—the last being particularly surprising given that they were traditionally left-wing party supporters (Birenbaum et al. 1996: 349). To cater to their new supporters, Le Pen and the FN began to actively solicit workers. For example, during the large public sector workers' strike, Mégret and other activists visited workers at the Moulinex plant in Mamers to show their support (Perrineau 1998: 47–48). In 1995 and 1996, the FN also became involved in the syndicate movement by founding two unions: one for police officers and one for prison guards (Perrineau 1998: 47–48).

In the 1997 legislative elections, the FN continued to rise, attracting about one million new or former supporters (Williams 2006: 85). The party received 15.24 % of the vote and was considered to be the third most important political force in France (DeClair 1999: 104).[31] It appeared that it had become a serious contender in French political life (Berezin 2007: 133). Only 15 years after its first electoral success in Dreux in 1983, the FN was beginning to challenge the mainstream parties, the PS and the RPR. Over two decades, the party had progressed from the fringes to the centre of national politics in spite of an onslaught of organizational and institutional challenges.

2.6 Crisis and Renewed Success

The FN's rise in electoral fortune and popular perception was (temporarily) crushed in December 1998, when the internal struggles between party leader Jean-Marie Le Pen and his de facto number two, Bruno Mégret, came to the fore. These struggles had begun in 1995, when Mégret officially criticized the strategic orientation of the FN (Dézé 2012: 125). As a contender to replace Le Pen as party president, Mégret developed permanent ties with other right-wing parties to enhance the role of the FN within French politics. This strategy resembled that of Gianfranco Fini, leader of the National Alliance party in Italy, who participated in Berlusconi's government. However, Le Pen rejected this approach; he was not interested in alliances and wanted to stay on the far-right fringe (Gauthier 2009: 391). Mégret's more moderate stance also did not sit well with the party's hard-core nationalists, who

---

[30]In addition to anti-immigration and security measures, Le Pen's campaign planks included the promise to create a Sixth Republic to replace the scandal-plagued institutions of the Fifth Republic (DeClair 1999: 97–100).

[31]In a by-election in February, Catherine Mégret won 52.5 % of the vote to become mayor of Vitrolles (Williams 2006: 88).

preferred ideological purity to political expediency (DeClair 1999: 163). This strategic dispute between Le Pen and Mégret continued into the party convention in Strasbourg in 1997, providing the image of a rather divided party.

The conflict over isolationism versus alliances with the mainstream right aggravated the rivalry between Le Pen and Mégret (Williams 2006: 87). Tensions peaked over the nominations in the 1999 European elections. After Le Pen physically assaulted socialist candidate Aline Paulevast during a campaign event in Mantes-la-Jolie in May 1997, a French court suspended his civic rights for 2 years. Consequently, he could not run in the 1999 European elections and had to withdraw his name (Dézé 2012: 115). Mégret was next in line to occupy the top position on the FN's list. However, Le Pen nominated his wife, Jany, as the chief candidate for the 1999 European elections and not Mégret. When criticized by Mégret and his supporters, Le Pen's response was scathing: "There is but one number in the FN; it is the number one" (Gauthier 2009: 392).

By mid-1998, Le Pen began to marginalize Mégret and his allies. He attacked Mégret's character and integrity, dismantled the youth group (*Renouveau Étudiant*) developed by Mégret, and demoted Mégret on the list for the 1999 European elections (Dézé 2012: 125). Finally, tensions between the opponents exploded at the party's national congress in December 1998, when Mégret stated that Le Pen had now become a handicap for the party (Gauthier 2009: 393) Mégret's fate, along with that of his allies, was sealed. The executive bureau, in which Le Pen supporters had the majority, voted to expel Mégret and his supporters from the party (Dézé 2012: 127). Only days later, Mégret formed a breakaway party called the National Republic Movement (MNR).

Le Pen's and Mégret's factions divided the far-right-wing vote in the 1999 European parliamentary elections: the FN received only 5.7 % of the votes (Berezin 2007: 137; Rydgren 2004: 18) and the MNR secured 3.3 % (Evans and Ivaldi 2005: 362; Dézé 2012: 130). Despite the MNR's defeat, the split was a considerable blow to the FN's ideological footing and organizational development: it lost not only its most prominent strategist but also close to half of its members. Yet, the FN did not suffer a permanent decline (Rydgren 2004: 21; Williams 2006: 87). In 2002, only 3 years after the party's internal crisis, and still deprived of a substantial portion of its caucus, Le Pen scored the best result in the party's history with an astonishing 16.9 % (4.8 million) of the national vote in the first round of the presidential election, bypassing the socialist candidate, Lionel Jospin, who won 16.2 % of the popular vote (Crépon 2012: 66). In the second round of the elections, the FN was able to capture 17.8 % of the votes cast (Rydgren 2004: 22; Goodliffe 2012: 137).

The 2002 election results made Le Pen the first leader of a nationalist party to accede to the second round of a presidential election in France. This election result was surprising even for FN members. The party was still recovering from the loss of at least half of its executive and activists, who either joined Mégret's MNR or, frustrated with this internal struggle, simply left politics altogether (Crépon 2012: 66). Several, mainly structural reasons accounted for the FN's surprisingly strong showing in the presidential elections. On the one hand, left-right "cohabitation" had accentuated a sentiment of confusion that allowed the FN to denounce the connections and personal ties between the political camps (Crépon 2012: 66). On the other hand, Chirac's campaign also indirectly served the FN's objectives, as he breached "frontist" themes related mainly to insecurity but also to immigration (de Lange 2007: 421).

However, this victory was not an unmitigated success for the FN, as it gave rise to ardent resistance by established parties and the French public. For instance, between the two rounds, defeated PS candidate Lionel Jospin went so far as to call for a block of Republicans of all stripes to unite against the nationalist threat presented by Le Pen (Crépon 2012: 65). Well beyond the second round of the presidential elections, the FN's credibility was seriously undermined by the media's anti-FN mobilization, which had a long-term impact on voters. Many FN members, such as Marie-Christine Arnautu,[32] believe not only that the party would have come to power were it not for the media's manipulation of the French public, but also that Le Pen's victory hurt the party in the long run (Crépon 2012: 68–69). Regardless of the party's future prospects, the anti-FN mobilization revealed that the party did not have the democratic legitimacy that it was desperately trying to achieve.

It was during this time that Jean-Marie Le Pen's daughter, Marine Le Pen, began to take a very active role in the party's activities. With the support of Louis Aliot[33] and FNJ leader Samuel Maréchal, she endeavoured to revitalize the FN's image for a new generation of supporters, the *"Génération Le Pen"*, which was founded by Jean Marie Le Pen's son-in-law, Samuel Maréchal, in 1998 (Crépon 2012: 56, 59). In 2000, she took up the presidency of this group of young FN supporters aiming to stop the "demonization" of the party. Her main goal was to improve the party's democratic legitimacy by expelling the more radical elements of *LePenism*. The 2007 electoral contests indicated that this "ideological" renewal was necessary. The party's vote share declined considerably; in the presidential elections, Jean-Marie Le Pen only received 10.75 % of the vote, and in the parliamentary elections the same year, the party's vote share dropped to less than 5 %. Yet, in subsequent elections, Marine Le Pen's strategy became influential within the FN and began to pay off (Williams 2006: 96).

Although Marine Le Pen and the party continued to campaign on nationalist-populist themes, they gradually refined the FN's discourse in a way that popularized its far-right ideas. This process of legitimization greatly contributed to the FN's ability to reverse its electoral slide. In the 2004 legislative regional and European elections, the party garnered 14.7 % and 9.8 % of the vote, respectively, whereas its moderate right-wing counterparts suffered defeat at the hands of the left on both occasions (Evans and Ivaldi 2005: 351). Bolstered by these electoral victories, Marine Le Pen continued to assume a "modernist" position that distanced her

---

[32]Marie-Christine Arnautu is presently the FN secretary-general for *l'Île-de-France* and member of the Political Bureau and Central Committee (Crépon 2012: 67).

[33]Louis Aliot joined the *Front National* in 1990. He acted as regional secretary (1998–1999) and has been regional councillor for Languedoc-Rousillon since 1998. Aliot is now FN vice-president, as well as member of the Executive Bureau, Political Bureau, and Central Committee (cf. Crépon 2012: 56–60).

from her father and softened the image of the FN (Dézé 2012: 139). Facing Bruno Gollnisch, representing the old image of the FN, in the internal elections to select Jean-Marie Le Pen's successor as president of the FN, Marine Le Pen incorporated this new image. Her *dédiabolization* (de-demonization) strategy was rewarded (Dézé 2012: 141; Kling 2012: 119). On January 16, 2011, she was voted in as the new president of the FN with 67.65 % support (11,546 votes); Gollnisch received 32.35 % support (5522 votes) (Dézé 2012: 141). Despite the discontent expressed by a few party members from the older generation who felt slighted, the transition occurred with astonishingly little tribulation, both within the FN and in the media (Kling 2012: 119).

2.7 The FN Under Marine Le Pen

So far, Marine Le Pen's *dédiabolization* strategy has proved successful not only internally but also externally in the electoral market (Coomarasamy 2011). She emerged as a strong candidate and rallied supporters under the slogan *Rassemblement Bleu Marine* in the 2012 presidential election (Goodliffe 2012: 137). Her platform mixed her fathers' signature issues of immigration, security, and national identity with a strong populist leftist message that included wage increases for workers and the re-nationalization of France.

The FN's campaign was a success; in the first round, Marine Le Pen received 18.03 % of the vote—an increase of almost 8 % from the results obtained by her father in 2007 (10.44 %). Although she did not come in second, as her father had done in 2002, she received 896,000 more votes than he had 10 years before. In the ensuing 2012 legislative elections, the FN received a total of 13.77 % of the votes (compared with 4.29 % in 2007) and won 2 seats in the National Assembly (Hewlett 2012: 414; Shields 2013: 189). The 2012 elections also marked the first time that the party managed to make significant gains in rural France and in the suburbs of large towns and cities (Hewlett 2012: 415).

The "new" *Front National* not only experienced a political revival in its appropriation of France's extreme-far-right space, it also gained more respectability in the eyes of the French public. In particular, Marine Le Pen's efforts to rebrand the party succeeded in modifying the opinion of a significant portion of the French population. Polls showed a decrease in the number of people who considered the FN a "danger" from 70 %, in 2002, to 53 %, in 2012 (TNS-Sofres 2012a). Another poll indicated that a slight majority of respondents saw the FN as "a party like the others" (TNS-Sofres 2012b). Finally, in a third poll, almost as many respondents felt that Marine Le Pen represented "a patriotic right attachment to traditional values" (41 %) as felt that she represented the "nationalist and xenophobic extreme right" (43 %) (TNS-Sofre 2012c).

In 2014, the FN tide continued to swell. In the March municipal elections, the FN won 12 towns and elected 1534 councillors—its best result ever on the local level. Most notable were its wins in Frejus, the 7th district in Marseille, and Hénin-

Beaumont (Laubacher 2014). In the European elections in May 2014, the FN success was even more pronounced. Winning an astonishing 25 % of the popular vote, the FN became the first party in France, passing the two moderate parties, the PS and the UMP, by several percentage points (the UMP came in second, with 20.8 % of the popular vote, and the PS came in third, garnering only 14 % of the vote). In total, the FN sent 24 deputies to Brussels and Strasbourg, making it not only the strongest party in France, but also the most successful radical right-wing party in Europe (*Ministère de l'Intérieur* 2014). In the 2015 departmental elections, the FN won 25.2 % of the vote, thus confirming its result in the 2014 European elections. In the December 2015 regional elections, the FN saw yet another moderate boost in its vote share, which stood at 27.9 %. However, this success plateaued in the second round. Although it elected regional councillors in all metropolitan regions, the FN garnered only 19 % of the vote in this second tour (*Ministère de l'Intérieur* 2015b).

It would be wrong to overestimate the electoral success of the FN; the European elections in 2014, as well as the 2015 departmental and regional elections, took place in the context of an ongoing economic crisis, record high unemployment, record low support for President Hollande, and internal conflicts within the centre-right-wing party, the UMP. In this context, there is the possibility that some voters used these second-order elections to direct their anger against the mainstream parties and their inability to resolve the economic, political, and social crises that France has been facing (Pertusot and Rittelmeyer 2014). This scenario is even more likely when we consider that electoral participation hit a record low: less than 50 % of the French electorate cast a ballot in the European elections and in the first round of the departmental and regional elections.

Nevertheless, it would also be wrong to underestimate the FN's success. The Front capitalized on the favourable structural conditions on the ground; Le Pen and her party convinced one out of four voters to support them. The party has also doubled its membership over the past three to 4 years. With over 80,000 dedicated members and a (latent) support base of around five million French voters, the party is well equipped to continue to play an important role in French politics. However, there are also some potential spoilers, which might keep it from continuing to rise in the polls and public opinion. In addition to the structural conditions, Marine Le Pen is having an open fight with Jean-Marie Le Pen over the strategic orientation of the party, and the former leader is continually challenging her leadership. In fact, after reiterating his anti-Semite statements and (partial) denial of the Holocaust, Jean-Marie Le Pen has become more and more of a problem to his daughter. In the light of some internal turmoil and fights, the latter has (temporarily) expelled the former from the party. Although Jean-Marie Le Pen is contesting this expulsion and the two leaders are engaged in some nasty battles, this tumult has not hurt the FN. Throughout 2015, the party continued to score high in opinion polls. According to the Ifop representative survey conducted on September 3 and 4, 2015, Marine Le Pen is credited with a near-record 29 % of vote intentions. There is also no sign of a mass exodus of FN members. Hence, the FN is likely to continue to play a major role in French politics in the years to come—although how major a role is up for debate.

In this book, I want to put the recent success of the FN into perspective. What, if anything, has changed in the supply side of right-wing support and activism between Jean-Marie Le Pen and Marine Le Pen? To what degree have the FN's programme and ideology changed? Is there some real shift to the centre, or has the FN just repackaged its slogans differently, or is there no programmatic change at all? These questions have strong repercussions for the demand side of activism. How have the membership and the voters changed? Who are the millions of new voters and tens of thousands of new members? Why do they support the FN? These questions are of utmost importance if we want to understand the party and its electoral successes. By discussing the change (or lack thereof) in the party's ideology between Marine Le Pen and Jean-Marie Le Pen, the leadership styles and composition of the party elites of the two leaders, the party's membership before and after the leadership transition, and the FN voters under Marine Le Pen and Jean-Marie Le Pen, I provide answers to these questions in the following four chapters.

Chapter 3
The FN's Ideology Under Jean-Marie Le Pen and Marine Le Pen

> In the history of human mankind, there is no example of peaceful and durable coexistence between different ethnic and religious communities (Mégret, quoted in Crépon 2006: 65).

For over 30 years, the FN has provided its members, sympathizers, and voters with a simplified picture of how the world is and how it should be. According to the traditional FN rhetoric, French society is tainted by foreign influences and lax governmental public security policies and oppressed by the dictates of European integration and economic globalization. The FN embeds these flaws in an ethnocentric worldview that has it that the nation should be reserved for citizens who share the same ethnicity, culture, religion, and history (Hainsworth 2008: 12). In practice, this worldview translates into a political discourse that advances positions against foreigners and immigrants, who are often linked to unemployment, public insecurity, and welfare chauvinism (thus, social programmes should exclusively benefit a nation's "own" people [cf. Eatwell 2000: 413]). Did this worldview change with Marine Le Pen's ascension to the FN presidency in 2011? This is the general question that I want to answer in this chapter.

The word *dédiabolisation*, which could be translated into English as demonization, is at the centre of Marine Le Pen's strategy and also at the centre of this chapter. Despite the fact that Marine Le Pen has used the term since 2007, her *dé diabolisation* strategy gained prominence during the internal campaign for the FN presidency in 2011. She used the term to distinguish herself from her internal rival, Bruno Gollnisch, whom she characterized as the representative of an old generation of activists with extremist doctrines (Almeida 2013). In contrast to Gollnisch, she presented herself as the new face of the radical right—a face that is more feminine and more republican, and that abstains from making overtly racist comments. Using Sargent's (1972: 2) now-famous definition of ideological change, I evaluate in this chapter whether this strategic reorientation should be interpreted as a narrative shift in the FN's vision of the state of society or simply a superficial makeover. In other words, can the time after 2011 be considered a process of modernization with the goal of gaining the party republican legitimacy?

I aim to answer these questions in a three-step process. First, I summarize the old ideology of the FN based on party programmes from 2006 to 2008. Then, I juxtapose those programmes against current FN programmes, underlining differences and commonalities between the party's "old" and "new" image and programme. Finally, I analyse the themes and ideological positions of three sets of 100 press releases, which I retrieved from the FN website in August–September 2012, August–September 2013, and August–September 2014. The analysis of these press releases further highlights the themes and positions that the FN has advanced since Marine Le Pen took control of the party in 2011 and whether these themes and positions have been fundamentally different from those advanced previously. In conclusion, in an effort to determine if there is coherence in the themes advanced by the FN, I evaluate the positions taken by regional chapters and the ideological proposals presented by the FN youth movement, the *Front National de la Jeunesse* (FNJ), between 2011 and 2014, and then I compare these positions with the official national rhetoric.

3.1 The FN's Ideology Under Jean-Marie Le Pen

The FN under Jean-Marie Le Pen officially operated within the constitutional arena; the party accepted the democratic institutions and procedures of the Fifth Republic but opposed liberal features such as guarantees for minority rights, checks on executive authority, social equality, and multiculturalism. As is typical for radical right-wing parties, immigration was at the centre of the programme. Many features of the FN programme, including social and public security and the labour market, were built around the immigration theme. The party's anti-immigration stance was complemented by other traditional characteristics of radical right-wing parties, including authoritarianism, anti-egalitarianism, and a focus on national sovereignty (see, e.g. Art 2011; Balent 2012).

3.1.1 Immigration

As is typical for a radical right-wing party, the FN under Jean-Marie Le Pen used anti-immigration or xenophobia as its defining feature (cf. Van Der Brug et al. 2005; Hainsworth 2008). Immigration was the central theme running through the FN's political programme for the 2007 presidential election. Moreover, most policy briefs published around that time tackled the immigration theme. Le Pen's 2007 presidential programme starts with an attack on immigration (*Le Front National* 2007: 5). According to the FN, in 2007, the annual cost of immigration was 60 billion Euros; 70 % of France's prison population was composed of individuals of foreign origin, when both legal and illegal immigrants were counted; 95 % of foreigners entered France without a work contract; and 50 % of social welfare beneficiaries were foreigners. After listing "the facts about immigration", the FN's platform

3.1 The FN's Ideology Under Jean-Marie Le Pen

clearly linked immigration to public insecurity, national identity, social security, and the labour market. This connection between immigration and social vices and problemmes was also present in most of the party's other policy briefs and programmatic documents published around 2007.

3.1.1.1 Immigration and Public Insecurity

Throughout its history, the FN has considered immigration a major source of pubic insecurity. This link also resonated in the 2007 presidential programme. For example, on page 8, the FN wrote, "the overrepresentation of immigrants in crime and criminality is a fact". Elsewhere, it deplored a multiplication of crimes against white people and lamented that these crimes against traditional French nationals are neither adequately listed in official documents nor correctly discussed in politics and society (Vox-FN 2006). To curb this natural aura of insecurity and criminal activity caused by immigration and multiculturalism, the FN advocated a policy of zero tolerance. Measures targeted directly against its scapegoat population, foreigners, included the dismantling of criminal organizations within immigrant networks and the prompt deportation of foreigners convicted of a crime (*Le Front National* 2008b).

3.1.1.2 Immigration and Social Security

The FN also decried the exploitation of social benefits by foreign nationals. According to the FN programme, immigrants (illegal and legal) were taking advantage of the social welfare system and other advantages that they "can't find in their home countries" (*Le Front National* 2007: 13).[34] The party claimed that massive immigration had triggered both a contributory deficit in social security and an increase in expenditures on healthcare and pensions, among other things. According to the FN, this increased pressure on the system placed a dramatic financial burden on "each French person, whose taxes ultimately funded the immigrants" use and abuse of the French system. Solutions would therefore include reserving benefits for the French, and "suppression of familial social benefits for non-nationals" (*Le Front National* 2008c). Throughout the late 2000s, and thereafter, the FN summarized these suggestions under the catchword "national preference". Whenever possible, nationals should be given preference, and this principle should be included in the French Constitution (*Le Front National* 2007: 53). In fact, according to official FN documentation, *la préférence nationale* ought to apply to the allocation of social housing, the payment of social benefits, and the posting of public sector jobs.

---

[34]See also Déclair (1999: 127) for an earlier description of how the FN links immigration to abuse of the social system.

3.1.1.3 Immigration and National Identity

The FN under Jean-Marie Le Pen was also very strong on both inciting fears about globalization and Europeanization and capitalizing on these concerns. In the FN's view, immigration, Europeanization, and the spread of neoliberal ideology undermined France's national identity (LaMontagne and Stockemer 2010: 43).[35] In its programme, it cited statistics on declining numbers of theatre audiences, visitors to national monuments, and moviegoers in order to create an image of cultural decline. Descriptions of the "deplorable conditions" of French monuments and the vulnerability of France's undefended musical heritage reinforced this image of decay (*Le Front National* 2007: 37–39). The party not only blamed the state for this cultural disintegration but opined that "for France to remain France, the French people must remain masters of their own home" (*Le Front National* 2008a). In fact, the party stated that massive immigration directly leads to a feeling of rootlessness:

> When women and men of different ethnic and religious backgrounds mix, immigrant nationals find themselves uprooted, severed from their traditions, just like the French living in the immigrant neighbourhoods who feel like foreigners in their own country (*Le Front National* 2008a).

3.1.1.4 Immigration and the Labour Market

The FN also linked immigration to the economy, even though this link was probably less direct in the 2007 presidential programme than were the other three themes. In the programme, Jean-Marie Le Pen and the FN proposed to cut all unemployment benefits (the revenu minimum d'insertion) for those who did not have a right to contribution-based benefits. The FN also proposed that foreigners pay higher contributions for their unemployment benefits, because of their statistically higher chances of being unemployed (*Front National* 2007: 38). Similar to its platform for the social sector, the party further proposed to apply the national preference to all public sector jobs: all public sector employment contracts should be given to French nationals, if at all possible. Finally, the party lamented that the majority of immigrants came to France for economic rather than political reasons. According to the FN programme, these newcomers were not competitive in the labour market; only 1 out of 20 immigrants that arrived in France were able to secure employment before arriving in the country. Although the connection between immigration and high unemployment was rather indirect in the FN 2007 official party programme, it was made clearer elsewhere. For example, the FN stated in 2006 in a thematic position paper, "Massive and uncontrolled immigration takes more

---

[35]"Immigration, globalization, and Europeanization have liquidated the natural and spiritual roots of France's culture. The French citizens have to liberate themselves from this totalitarian conformity of their culture" (*Le Front National* 2006).

than 1 million jobs away from the French and severely punishes our economy by imposing costs of over 300 billion francs" (*Le Front National* 2006).

3.1.2 Other Features of the FN Programme

Nearly by definition, anti-pluralism, anti-egalitarianism, cultural monism, anti-globalization, and anti-Europeanism followed closely from the party's firm anti-immigration platform. First, as a key policy proposal, the term "national preference" was referred to and explained six times in the party's 2007 presidential programme. Second, anti-globalization, anti-liberalism, and anti-Europeanism featured rather strongly in the document. In addition to being linked to immigration, globalization, liberalism, and Europeanism were pegged as culprits for cultural and economic decline: in cultural terms, neo-liberalism led to the uniformity of the French lifestyle. Foreign influences destroyed France's heritage and traditions. Economically, the FN deplored the relocation of French businesses abroad, unfair foreign competition, and the deindustrialization of France. As a solution, the party proposed the re-establishment of national sovereignty and the protection of French companies. Moreover, it affirmed that it would take France out of the European Union if voted into power (*Le Front National* 2007: 59).

References to authoritarianism, as another traditional component of radical right-wing ideology (Mudde 2010, 2012), also featured quite prominently in the FN 2007 presidential programme. For instance, to boost public security, the FN strongly favoured giving more power to the police and advocated stronger punishments for petty and major crimes. Concrete measures included a policy of zero tolerance against criminals and the reintroduction of the death penalty. The FN also wanted to ensure that the police and the military were respected as guardians of the French nation and aimed to provide better funding and equipment to the military. Moreover, the party proclaimed that if elected it planned to leave NATO and insisted that the French military should exclusively defend French interests (*Le Front National* 2007: 31–34). In a different policy field, institutional reform, the FN favoured strengthening presidential prerogatives; measures included setting the electoral term for a president back to 7 years.

However, two characteristics, currently associated with radical right-wing parties—populism and anti-elitism—despite being milestones in early campaigns, featured, if at all, only marginally in the FN 2007 programme. In fact, it seems that in the late years of being the party's president, Jean-Marie Le Pen softened his populist tone and rhetoric, which was a cornerstone of the FN's strategy in the 1980s and 1990s. Rather than being populist, the 69-page 2007 election programme was written in a rather scientific way. Throughout the document, the FN provided many statistics to back up its claims. For example, for every policy measure proposed in its programme, the party offered estimates on how much that measure would cost the state or the taxpayer. However, aside from the proposal to hold referenda, no populist measures were on the agenda. There was no link to the national community as a catchword to reuniting the people, nor was there any proposal on how the FN would help low-income classes or workers cope with growing unemployment and social hardship. In addition, Jean-Marie Le Pen's name was not mentioned once in the document. Even its title page was very neutral. The title, "Presidential Election 2007, Program", is placed against a background showing a group of people in front of a landscape.

Anti-elitism, which is often linked to or seen as an integral part of populism, also did not feature prominently in the FN 2007 electoral programme. As he did for populism, Jean-Marie Le Pen used his anti-elitist rhetoric less strongly in the final years of his presidency. For example, there was only one reference to the "UMPS", a label that the FN used for years to describe what it calls the corrupt elites of the two mainstream parties, UMP and PS. The words "corruption" and "elites" were not used at all. In fact, the FN was presented as anti-elitist only in the sense that it rejected all the international forces (such as the European Union, multi-national corporations, and international banks) that, according to the party, threatened the well-being of France's economy, culture, and identity.

3.2 The FN's Ideology Under Marine Le Pen

Since Marine Le Pen took the party's reins in 2011, the FN has published only one programme: its 2012 presidential platform. Probably aiming to keep its platform clear and simple, the party did not publish any policy briefs after 2010. The 2012 electoral platform reintroduces many of the themes in Jean-Marie Le Pen's presidential project. For immigration, anti-Europeanism, welfare chauvinism, public security, and national identity, the FN suggests the same solutions as it did in 2007. In fact, a closer look at the document gives the impression that some of the proposed policies in the current FN programme have become even more severe. This applies in particular to proposals geared towards the target population, immigrants, for whom the programme advocates more restrictive measures in the social, economic, and security fields. Thus, the content has not changed, but the same cannot be said for the form and set-up of the message. Rather than being pseudo-intellectual, the message is strongly populist in the new programme (see Krastev 2007: 57 and Liang 2007: 3–6 for a description of populism).

The FN presents its leader, Marine Le Pen, at the centre of the programme, as the personification of the general will of the people. The cover page of the programme shows a close-up illustration of the FN president, placing her at the centre of the first page, presenting her as a leader and the FN as a party whose main objective is to defend the French nation and its people. The programme is titled "My Project, for France and for the French people, and Marine Le Pen, the voice of the people, the spirit of France". From the first page, the FN is equated with the name of Marine Le Pen; the programme contains 10 references to her and no reference to the FN as a party. She is directly juxtaposed against the corrupt French elites; she is presented as the personification of change, the beginning of a new chapter in French history. In fact,

3.2 The FN's Ideology Under Marine Le Pen

the party distinguishes itself from the other parties through her. For example, on page 3, the text reads,

> There are only two choices to make France competitive again: either reduce wages and dismantle the social protection system—this is the choice of the "UMPS"; or act on our money and refuse the drastic austerity plans—this is the choice of Marine Le Pen.

In addition to raising Marine to the position of the saviour of France, the programme directly addresses lower- and working-class people, the part of the population who probably feels the most alienated by political developments at home and abroad. To appeal to these masses, the programme is clear and simple. It is only 16 pages long. It appeals to the common sense of the electorate and advocates straightforward policy solutions. The major preoccupations of the working and lower-middle classes—salaries, purchasing power, and social and public security—are at its core. To convince the popular classes that neo-liberal policies are outdated, the FN proposes populist measures, including a significant rise in modest incomes and pensions, protection of the French economy against foreign influences, and punishment of all abusers of social security in France.

Immigration, the central topic in Jean-Marie Le Pen's platform, is directly referred to only in the middle of the FN programme, sandwiched between the party's economic platform, which the party presents up front, and the party's agenda in the social, cultural, and foreign realms. However, this less prominent placement within the FN platform does not make immigration a less important topic. To the contrary, throughout the programme the FN asks for solidarity among the French people. Those who are ruining the economy and the social system—foreigners—are not included in the national community and the system of solidarity that the party aims to create. Consequently, non-nationals should not benefit from the same generous welfare system measures as French nationals do. Chauvinistic welfare measures proposed by the FN include the elimination of all pensions for foreigners who have not worked in France for at least 10 years, and the suppression of all family benefits if the parents do not have French nationality.

In fact, the solutions that the FN proposes with regard to immigration are in no way less radical than the measures proposed 5 years prior. In the programme, there are traditional FN proposals such as the expulsion of all illegal immigrants, a change in citizenship right (French citizenship should no longer be granted to those who are born in France, but only to newborns whose parents have the French nationality), and measures fostering strict regulations regarding new immigration. In addition, the programme contains new proposals, such as the application of the national preference not only in the public sector but also in the private sector, and the implementation of especially harsh punishment for racist crimes committed against white people.

The FN platform on other topics, such as the organization of the state, the role of the armed forces in French society, the strengthening of the judicial system, and the role of French culture in society, mimics the propositions made in 2007. A topic that gains more attention in Marine le Pen's project is the notion of *laïcité*. The party dedicates one of the 16 pages in its programme to the topic. What comes to the fore in the FN's discussion of the term is that the concept's republican meaning—the regulation of the relationship between state and church and the guarantee of independence of the former from the latter—is depleted in the FN's usage of it. Under the banner of *laïcité*, the FN opposes affirmative action programmes and communitarianism. It also decries the spread of Islam, which, according to the party, is an inherently dangerous religion that does not respect the separation between state and church. Hence, the FN instrumentalizes the republican term *laïcité* to oppose all forms of community other than the nation (see also Almeida 2013: 172).

Throughout its programme, the party not only tries to capitalize on the latent social and cultural turmoil and the widespread feeling of dislocation within the French population, but it also presents three culprits for France's economic and social decay. The first is the European Union and the European currency, the Euro. According to the FN, the Euro has not kept any promise in the 10 years of its existence: it stands for the exploding prices, unemployment, outsourcing, and public debt. Second is the dominance of the international banking system, under which France is suffocating. To liberate France from the yoke of the supremacy of international banks, the FN wants to re-establish the franc and gain control over its own monetary policies. The third is France's political, social, and cultural elites. The party juxtaposes the pure people, on the one hand, against the corrupt elite, on the other hand. This juxtaposition is probably most pronounced when, within her 2012 platform, Marine Le Pen links the lavish lifestyle of France's political elites to France's debt crisis. For example, in order to fix the public finances, she promises to rein in the sumptuous expenses and excessive reimbursements from which the French political elites benefit. She also links corrupt practices to the "UMPS", indicating that members of both major parties milk the system for their own benefit.

Moreover, the FN programme has an undertone of crisis. France's current state of affairs is described not as an ordered policy, but as a situation of economic, social, and political chaos and decline. Semantically, the programme contains the words "rupture" and "break-up" on several occasions, as an indication that the party wants to break with the current liberal policies. Instead of the current regime, it wants to implement a populist form of democracy, based on the general will of the people. As a rhetorical device, the FN also uses war language. In the programme are phrases such as "small neighbourhood markets must be defended against multinational corporations" and "social abuse will be combated". This strong language reinforces the message that the party is "at war" with the system and the actors that represent it.

In sum, in the programme, the FN and Marine Le Pen present themselves as outsiders to the political system; they see themselves as an alternative to mainstream politics and, more generally, to the political system. The party proposes a form of populist democracy, a form of government that assembles French citizens under the banner of nationalism. It aims at strengthening the authority of the state (e.g. the police and the judicial system) and identifies several culprits for the social, political, and cultural decay that France has been experiencing (e.g. the national and international political and economic elites). By proposing radical measures in the areas of immigration, public security, and the organization of the state, the FN not only breaks with republican taboos of the Fifth Republic, it also presents itself as a fresh political force that actually aims to represent the common people. Marine Le Pen is at the centre of this project; she presents herself as the political representative of the people, the embodiment of the popular will, the saviour of France.

3.2.1 The FN Ideology in Its Press Releases

Except for some renewed emphasis on populism and anti-elitism, the FN's 2012 presidential programme portrays a picture of continuity rather than change. To complement this analysis and to obtain a more complete picture of the FN's ideology outside of its official electoral platform, I have analysed 300 press releases, which the FN published on its website in 2012, 2013, and 2014. For each year, I used the September 30 as the cut-off date and analysed the 100 most recent press releases after this date. In short, these press releases mimic and mirror the propositions that the FN put forward in its 2012 electoral programme. As is the case in Marine Le Pen's 2012 election programme, most, if not all, of the pieces are written in a populist tone that not only disparages the parties in the system but also portrays hope and a vision for a different society. In addition, the press releases portray the image that (electoral) victory is close. For instance, the FN speaks of a terrible anxiety in the political caste, which is confronted with a responsible and courageous policy whose electoral force makes the system tremble (*Le Front National* 2013a).

Table 3.1 summarizes the major themes expressed in these press releases: the economy, social security, and immigration are at the core of the FN's message. Both policy domains are shaped by the notion of resentment politics and by the party's striving to transform the system. For example, Florian Philippot (2014a), the FN's general manager, advocates for a complete overhaul of the French economic system: France must "find a national currency adapted to its economy, regain control of its budget, set up smart border protection and a policy of economic nationalism in the context of a strategic state". Further, confirming the strong populist appeal from its 2012 programme, the FN portrays itself in several dozen press releases as the defender of workers and state employees against elitist interests that are corrupting the nation. Firmly opposing the austerity measures that have been imposed by the last two French governments (the Sarkozy and Hollande governments), the party considers the UMP and the PS to be a threat to the financial security and prosperity of the French population. In an effort to affirm its ethno-socialist or populist standpoint, several press releases also attack the

Table 3.1 The themes covered in FN press releases

	Economy and social security	Immigration	Public safety	National identity	Europe	Other
Percent	26	21	14	12	10	17

government for not spending enough to help lower-income members of society and the unemployed. Again, these proposals are framed in an "us versus them" mentality; only the French unemployed, pensioners, and low-income classes should benefit from national solidarity.

The second-most cited theme in the FN's press releases is the party's signature theme, immigration. The FN not only demands that the trend of "massive" and "uncontrolled" immigration be reversed and illegal immigrants be immediately expelled but also appeals to the idea of social patriotism (the idea that French nationals must form a unified front against the abusers of the system, legal and illegal immigrants). Immigration is further associated with an "alarming communitarianism" and held responsible for "the crisis of assimilation" in France (Aliot 2013). In 2014, Marine Le Pen summarized that legal and illegal immigration can be curtailed only through "the exit from the Schengen area, the return to permanent national frontiers, and the automatic expulsion of apprehended clandestine immigrants". Another element in the press releases is that members of the FN flip the meaning of racism and xenophobia and portray French citizens as victims of "anti-French racism" and "foreign preference" policies. For example, Bruno Gollnisch (2013) describes *le racisme anti-blanc, anti-chrétien et anti-français* as the most common form of racism on French soil.

A third recurring theme, public safety, is framed very traditionally. For instance, the FN uses insecurity to advance socio-authoritarian policies as a means of remedying the ineffectiveness of the judicial system in France. Fabien Engelmann (2014), the mayor of Hayange, describes the "lax justice system that releases offenders" and admonishes the government to "have a little more discernment in the choices that govern the daily lives of millions of French". The policies that the FN advances in the area of public security are no different from what it proposed in the past. They include the deportation of convicted foreign nationals to their home countries, the imposition of stricter laws, the dismantling of immigrant crime networks, and the closure of religious institutions fostering communitarianism, fundamentalist thought, and terror.

One in four press releases focuses on two topics, national identity and Europe. As it does in its programme, the FN supports both state nationalism and ethnic nationalism. Pertaining to state nationalism, the party sees the state as the main form of organization regulating all aspects in life. With regard to ethnic nationalism, the FN maintains that the state should be composed of people sharing the same blood, culture, religion, and heritage. To glorify the uniting force of French identity, the FN continues to use populist language, juxtaposing the French nation against out-groups such as foreigners and international and European institutions.[36] Furthermore, the FN portrays the picture that France is suffocating from servitude and fiefdom to an all-mighty European Union. For example, Florian Philippot (2014b) accuses the French government of "being more preoccupied with obeying orders

---

[36]The separation of French society into an "in-group" and an "out-group" has been a recurring strategy over the decades (see Evans and Ivaldi 2005: 354; Minkenberg and Perrineau 2007: 32).

from its Brussels and German masters than responding to everyday concerns of the French people".

Finally, topics listed under the rubric "other" include France's role in the international sphere, education policies, and the FN's self-victimization. With regard to the international sphere, the FN advocates that France must regain its international influence, gain independence from the United States, and intervene strategically. Again, the party's propositions are framed in a populist undertone (e.g. the FN accuses the "UMPS" of having been on their knees when dealing with the United States for the past 20 years [Philipot 2013]). In education, the FN advocates that excellence and hard work be rewarded over the promotion of procrastination. Thematically, the FN pushes for a more nationalistic history programme that encourages students to learn about the great French philosophers, statesmen, and scientists. Finally, in a total of nine press releases, the FN deliberately presents itself as a victim of the main parties—which are considered crooked, corrupt, and incompetent—thus renewing its anti-elitist character.

3.2.2 The FN Ideology by Regional FN Chapters and the FNJ

Whether looking at the official party programme or at press releases, so far I find a continuation of the FN's message, albeit packaged somewhat differently with a more populist and more anti-elitist undertone. The leitmotif of the FN programme, populism, also guides many of the statements and slogans found on regional websites. Be it "Toward a patriotic revolution with Marine Le Pen" (*Le Front National* 81), "Defend our colours" (*Le Front National de l'Indre* 2013), or "*Les Jeunes avec Marine*" (*Le Front National de la Jeunesse* 2011), the FN speaks directly to the people and invites them to join its project. Analogous to its national program, the party presents itself as the sole defender of popular democracy against corrupt national and international institutions. To denounce globalization and Europeanization at once, the FN often uses the term "euro-globalization". For example, the FNJ speaks about the European project in terms of globalization:

> Globalization without borders and without protection of any kind, one of thoughtlessness and irresponsibility, led by a very small few, considerably weakens all that is wonderful about our country. (*Le Front National de la Jeunesse* 2013a)

The reference to the "small few" describes French politicians of the mainstream parties, the "UMPS", who in their elitist bubble are absolved of the sorrows, concerns, and will of the masses. In fact, according to the FN rhetoric, the French elites push a project that will lead to the economic, social, and political decay of France.

Probably even more overtly nationalist, the regional chapters of the FN make a direct link between the party's nativist ideology and its attitudes towards immigration. This ethnocentric message abounds in slogans such as those made by France

Jamet (2012), FN president for Languedoc-Roussillon: "France, love it or leave it". The link between immigration and Islam is also made more openly regionally than nationally. For example, the *Front National Loiret* (2014) states on its website that Muslim immigration severely threatens French secular values. Highlighting the social dimension of Islam, the *Front National Loire* (2014) finds that "Ramadan is a perversion of Lent". In its statement, this regional FN chapter describes the religious holiday as a "pathology" that leads to overconsumption and taxes the French healthcare system. This strong anti-Islam stance is echoed by the FNJ. For example, FNJ member Véronique Fornilli (2013) asks in a recent article if there is an Islam that is compatible with the French Republic.

The FN's socio-authoritarian themes are strongly promoted on the subnational level as well. In particular, FN councillors make frequent references to law and order, decrying a climate of insecurity. For instance, the *Front National Indre* has used the term "riffraff" (*racailles*) to describe petty criminals in the region (Colombier 2011). The *Le Front National de la Jeunesse* (2011) has also taken up the term riffraff as a catchword: "No riffraff in our neighbourhoods—No neighbourhoods for riffraff". In 2011, the *Front National Alpes-Maritime* used the slogan "Take Back Our Right to Security" to portray security as a fundamental human right—one that is currently being violated. Pushing for more public security, the *Front National de la Jeunesse en Alpes-Maritimes* (2013) complains about the daily and intolerable assaults in the region's public transportation system. Finally, talking about his riding in the South of France, FN affiliated National Assembly member. In 2013, Gilbert Collard deplores the climate of violence and insecurity in the vulnerable zones of Gard. In the press release, he particularly sympathizes with "honest inhabitants" who are allegedly exasperated and worried by the "increasing aggressions, harassment, and incivilities" (*Le Front National* 2013b).

The analysis of regional websites also makes it clear that the FN, at least at the grass-roots level, has not changed its position on homosexuality and the family. On both issues, the party remains traditionalist and conformist. As such, it rejects same-sex marriage and the adoption of children by same-sex couples. To highlight this position, deputy Marion Maréchal claimed that the law that the French parliament passed in early 2013 to allow same-sex marriage and adoption by same-sex couples "threatens the future and wellbeing of children" (*Le Front National* 2013c). Even more radical, Christophe Boudot, FN Secretary for Rhône-Alpes, described the legalization of same-sex marriage as a "forced march" towards the total abandonment of France's traditional values (*Le Front National Rhône* 2014).

3.2.3 Quo Vadis Dédiabolisation?

Although the term *dédiabolisation* has been extensively discussed in the media and academia, there are no signs in the FN programme that the party has moderated its message and become more republican (see also Dézé 2015). Rather than shifting towards less radicalism and towards a stronger adherence to the republican values of

3.2 The FN's Ideology Under Marine Le Pen

the Fifth Republic, the party has shifted towards ethno-socialism under Marine Le Pen (see also Reynie 2011). In fact, after originally abandoning its original neo-liberal agenda à la Thatcher and Reagan of the 1980s, which was based on low taxation and welfare retrenchments, the party has extended its anti-liberal profile to economic issues in the last two decades. Under Marine Le Pen, the state has become omnipresent; its role is to protect common people against the vices of neo-liberalism and immigration. The segment of the population that suffers the most from the economic crisis in France, workers and lower- and lower-middle-class people, are at the centre of the FN programme and rhetoric.

Consistent with the notion of populism, the FN brands itself as an anti-party (see Taggart 1995; Hainsworth 2000, 2008; Hooghe et al. 2002; Kriesi et al. 2008). It opposes the political, social, and economic system and all actors that represent France's Fifth Republic; it opposes economic and cultural globalization, Europeanization, the notion of European identity, multiculturalism, the mainstream political parties, and social, cultural, and academic elites. Adhering to this complete opposition perspective allows the party to present itself as a new outside political force that has not been corrupted by the power of the system. This policy stands in opposition to the notion of political liberalism and republicanism. Hence, there are no signs of deradicalization when it comes to the party's core message.

Yet the same cannot be said with regard to the form that the FN uses to present its message. There are three major differences between Jean-Marie Le Pen and Marine Le Pen. First, despite the fact that the party remains rooted in its ideological core, it presents itself as a republican party under Marine Le Pen. In contrast to her father, who never questioned the labels "extreme right" or "far-right", Marine Le Pen defines the party as a populist republican alternative and vows to fight anybody in court who labels her movement extreme right. She has repeatedly stated during press conferences that "we are absolutely not a rightist party; those who believe it make a colossal interpretation error". She further deplores that the FN is not treated as a party like others despite the fact that her movement is "neither right nor left", but, rather, that "she has radically different ideas from the PS and the UMP" (*La Libération* 2013). To underline her republican credentials, she has removed all references to figures of the French radical right in her speeches. Whereas her father often referenced Charles Maurras, Robert Brasilach, and Alexis Carrel, she cites Emile Zola, Jean Jaures, and Hannah Arendt in her speeches (see Almeida 2013).

Second, and with the exception of attacking Islam, Marine Le Pen has stopped making overtly racist and anti-Semitic statements. In contrast to her father, who periodically made racist, revisionist, or anti-Semitic declarations (and still does), such as describing the Holocaust as "a detail of history of the Second World War" (see Birenbaum 1992: 99), Marine Le Pen adheres to a republican rhetoric and expels anybody from the party who makes outright racist, anti-Semitic, or revisionist comments (Alduy and Wahnich 2015). She also loudly admonished her father when he adhered to his provocative and racist rhetoric. For example, when, referring to a couple of Jewish artists, he stated, "Listen, we'll deal with the lot of them in a batch next time", she made it clear that this statement does not represent the party line. She also labelled the remarks "regrettable", while publicly reminding her father that she was now in charge of the party (*L'Express* 2014). Because her admonishments have not borne any fruit, Marine Le Pen expelled her father from the party in the summer of 2015, when he continued to make anti-Semitic statements (see also Chap. 4).

Third, the FN presents itself as the defender of traditional republican concepts, including sovereignty and *laïcité*, even if it is just to promote its own ethnocentric positions. For example, it deplores the loss of sovereignty that French people face when confronted with an international conglomerate that includes supranational bodies such as the EU and international agreements such as the Lisbon Treaty, Schengen, and GATT. Similarly, it instrumentalizes the meaning of secularism or *laïcité* to promote its anti-Islamic rhetoric and propaganda (see Beauzamy 2013: 182). For example, Marine Le Pen refers to secularism as a means of defending individual rights and the common interest of the nation (Le Monde 2014a). In fact, her strongly racist and anti-Muslim comments, such as use of the term "occupation" to describe the presence of Muslims praying in the streets of France, are embedded in a republican discourse (see Shields 2013: 193).

3.2.4 The FN in 2015: Radical Right with a Softened Image

As of September 2015, it seems that the "new" *Front National*, under the leadership of Marine Le Pen, has seen a political revival that has allowed the party to position itself as the populist alternative to the mainstream parties, pejoratively labelled "UMPS". It is, in many respects, an anti-party: it rejects globalization, Brussels, Islamification, and France's political and social elites. Those who face an uncertain future in the current liberalized, globalized world, such as young individuals, pensioners, and blue-collar workers, are at the core of the FN's message (see also Gougou 2015).[37] To attract these low- and middle-income classes, the party promises wage increases for modest income earners, a drop in the retirement age to 60, the reindustrialization of France, and a "Buy French" obligation in public procurement (see also Goodliffe 2012: 137).

Under the leadership of Marine Le Pen, the FN also continues to push its signature theme, immigration, by linking it to social and public insecurity. The party's anti-immigrant discourse is further advanced as part of an original solution: greater national sovereignty (Coomarasamy 2011). Much like her father, Marine Le Pen portrays herself and the FN as the very embodiment of France, as the sole representative of the French people. However, while remaining faithful to the FN's signature themes and pushing its populist appeal, Marine Le Pen has also succeeded in softening the party's image by changing the tone of its message. She has broken with the provocative, insulting, and anti-Semitic rhetoric of the "old" FN

---

[37] For a description of the "losers of modernization" thesis, see Falter and Schumann (1988).

represented by Jean-Marie Le Pen. Without changing either the FN's ideology or its core positions, she has been successful in giving the party a new face—that of a more respectable party.

In fact, prominent members of the party had struggled for 25 years to make the FN's message respectable to the French people. Previous attempts, whether it was the now-famous slogan, *"Ni droite, ni gauche . . . Front National"*, which was first advanced in the 1980s by the then FNJ leader Samuel Maréchal; Bruno Mégret's attempts to soften the party's image and forge alliances with the mainstream right in the 1990s; or the foundation of *Génération Le Pen*, which aimed to give the FN a younger and more modern image, in the 2000s, all failed because of Jean-Marie Le Pen. He has always maintained that the FN's message must be different from that of the mainstream parties not only in its content but also in its form and delivery (2014b). Understanding that if the FN wants to be a serious contender in elections, it has to soften the presentation of its platform; Marine Le Pen has dedemonized the way the party presents its message. However, she has not changed any of the core ideological features, except for a re-emphasis on the party's populist turn. Nor has the FN has changed any of its policy proposals on immigration, identity politics, and public security, or its anti-elitist position.

However, the change in tone has enabled the party to cast off parts of its demonic image and manoeuvre its way into mainstream acceptability. Although it might not be easy to undo four decades as an authoritarian, xenophobic, dubiously democratic, anti-system party (Shields 2007: 315), the FN has become a party like other for the majority of French citizens (54 %, according to a representative opinion poll published in *Le Figaro* [2013]). In particular, the change in presentation of its message has allowed the FN to carve out political space for itself as a main contender in French politics.

Chapter 4
The FN's Leadership and Elites Under Jean-Marie Le Pen and Marine Le Pen

Aside from a radical right-wing ideological conception and programme, the FN's image (like any other party's image) depends to a large degree on leadership, party organization and the composition of the party elites, and relations with the media. These three supply-side factors exert a major influence on the image that a party cultivates among members, supporters, and the general public. When it comes to leadership, there is academic consensus that the quality of leadership of parties at either end of the ideological spectrum plays a central role in explaining their success or failure (Kessler and Freeman 2005: 265; Kitschelt 2007: 1194). In particular, there is general agreement in scholarly circles and in public opinion that most successful radical right-wing parties emphasize a highly exalted, personalist style of leadership (Mudde 2013: 1328). To what degree do the leadership styles of Jean-Marie Le Pen and Marine Le Pen fit this description? Are there differences between their leadership styles? Is one of them more charismatic than the other? I will try to answer these questions in the first part of this chapter. Second, I will discuss the composition of the party's elites, how they have helped structure the FN, and what relationship they have had with the respective leaders. Even for parties on the fringes, which see themselves as an alternative or new political force, media access and media relations are crucial. The FN is no exception to this rule. In the last part of the chapter, I explain how, although its relationship with the media was tense at times, the FN's electoral success under both Jean-Marie Le Pen and Marine Le Pen has been frequently linked to the FN's treatment in the media.

4.1 Leadership: Jean-Marie Le Pen Versus Marine Le Pen

4.1.1 Jean-Marie Le Pen

The charismatic leadership of Jean-Marie Le Pen is crucial to explaining the FN's trajectory from a marginal party in the 1970s to a major contender in French politics in the 1980s, 1990s, and 2000s. From the party's creation in 1972 to his retirement as party president in 2011, Jean-Marie Le Pen was the FN's face, its charismatic and personalist leader (Startin 2014). In 1972, as the party was being formed, he profited from the fact that the French radical right was far from coherent or unified. Instead, individuals who adhered to an extreme-right-wing ideology at the time were bound to the Second World War and colonial issues, Vichy France, and struggles around French Algeria, or to royalist or traditionalist-conservative Catholic beliefs (Perrineau 2014: 71–72). A strong, experienced leader with a distinct, or even authoritative, personality was necessary to unite these tendencies. Jean-Marie Le Pen fulfilled these criteria. He had the political credentials to unify diverse elements. He had entered the political arena in the 1950s with the Poujadist movement, gained parliamentary experience as the youngest deputy in the National Assembly, and made himself known as a highly qualified orator and as a tribune of the people (Mayer 1998: 5–6).

Soon after his election to the party presidency, Jean-Marie Le Pen became the sole face of the FN. Having consolidated his position, he governed his organization with an iron fist (Hainsworth and Mitchell 2000: 454). On the one hand, this allowed him to ensure some internal party discipline. He was successful in uniting one of the most fragmented political families and combining the many sensibilities within the FN (Lebourg and Beauregard 2012: 365). On the other hand, his iron fist prevented the party from diversifying at the leadership level. He never accepted any kind of challenge from other party members (Igounet 2014: 20) and used the tactics of expulsion and division to maintain control over the party (Lebourg and Beauregard 2012: 365). He also was not shy to expel very prominent figures from the party, most notably Bruno Mégret. After reorienting the party and receiving credit for some of its electoral successes at the time, Mégret challenged Le Pen's leadership style and programmatic choices in the late 1990s. After one of the ugliest leadership battles in recent French politics, he was expelled from the party in 1999.

Le Pen was the driving force of the FN for almost 40 years, and he considered the party his personal property (Bell 1994: 232). From the start, he designed the party on the model of a family business (Perrineau 2014: 61). In fact, he made no secret of his preference for promoting close family members within the party structure. He once famously stated, "I prefer my daughters to my cousins, my cousins to neighbours, my neighbours to strangers, and strangers to enemies" (quoted in Albertini and Doucet 2013: 103). Alongside Marine Le Pen, who today is undoubtedly the best-known representative of the Le Pen family in the party, several more of Jean-Marie Le Pen's relatives played an important role within the party, in particular during the 1990s. For instance, Samuel Maréchal, Le Pen's son-in-law, was a key player in the last few years of the twentieth century; he was very close to Le Pen and served as a kind of personal advisor to him. Most notably, he created one of the most important FN slogans to date: "Neither right, nor left: French!" (quoted in Igounet 2014: 333). Other Le Pen family members who played key roles in the FN hierarchy were Jean-Marie's second wife, Jany Le Pen; his other two daughters, Marie-Caroline and Yann Le Pen; and Yann's husband, Philippe Oliver (the last two fell into disgrace after supporting Bruno Mégret during the internal fights in 1998 and 1999 [Cohen and Péan 2012]).

Not only did Jean-Marie Le Pen have a distinct and autocratic leadership style, but he also used two separate strategies to communicate his message. First, he always tried to insinuate the FN's *créneaux porteurs*, or signature themes, immigration and law and order, into the political debate. He introduced these themes in a clear and straightforward way (e.g. "A million unemployed is a million immigrants too many" [quoted in Bariller and Timmermanns 1993]). At the same time, in his political speeches and interventions, he avoided more technical subjects such as specifics about the economy or the tax system, which were not necessarily the most fruitful topics for the FN (Lorien et al. 1985: 157). Second, he was a master of provocations that are generally referred to as *dérapages* (slips of the tongue). The most famous of these slips was his description of the Nazi gas chambers as a "detail" of history. Other of his controversial statements included that he believes "in the inequalities of races" and that the German occupation of France during the Second World War was not that inhumane after all (Nouvel Observateur 2009).

It is important to note that these kinds of provocations were not accidental; rather, they were always well planned by Le Pen in order "to project the extreme right's viewpoint in demotic language, deploying vivid images" (Bell 1994: 231). In Mathias's (2007: 37) view, an important part of what, in France, is called *l'effet Le Pen* is based on these provocations, which were a continuum in Le Pen's strategy since 1983. On the one hand, the indignant reactions and controversies that these statements provoked served his strategy of focusing the public debate on his own declarations. On the other hand, large parts of the French electorate developed a skeptical and contentious image of him—an image that Lebourg and Beauregard (2012) label *la marque Le Pen* (the Le Pen brand). In fact, his provocations made Jean-Marie Le Pen one of the most heartily disliked political figures in France, as he could at a stroke polarize opinions against him by driving away conservatives of the traditional right. At the same time, however, Le Pen's political blunders also brought him admirers, who always valued his candid behaviour. Whether he was liked or hated, Jean-Marie Le Pen always displayed some "magnetic attraction" that helped him reach out to a wider audience than the party itself could do (Bell 1994: 232). At least until 2002, the FN vote was mainly seen as a Jean-Marie Le Pen vote (Mayer 2002: 37), and the FN was equated with its co-founder.

4.1.2 Marine Le Pen

Despite the fact that Marine Le Pen's accession to the party leadership would probably not have been possible without her father (he supported her rise to the leadership to keep the party within family control), Marine Le Pen has tried to distance herself from her father's "rhetorical" leadership style (Alduy and Wahnich 2015). She was among the first members of the FN to see this style as an impediment to progress (Hainsworth and Mitchell 2000: 450). As early as 2004, she started to semantically distance herself from her father by introducing a softer image of the FN. For example, in her political discourse she promoted topics that have traditionally belonged to the left, such as the republic and secularism. She has also made some remarks critical of historical *LePenism*, including Jean-Marie Le Pen's rhetorical slips of the tongue (Igounet 2014: 386). In the development of her ideological positions, she was heavily inspired by the political strategies used by the Dutch radical leaders Pim Fortuym and Geert Wilders (Camus 2011: 156). Following the Dutch model, she has pushed a more human face of the radical right, condemning anti-Semitism, adopting gay-friendly positions, and presenting herself as a defender of the French secular republican model (Mayer 2013: 163).

Since becoming FN leader in 2011, not only has Marine Le Pen positioned herself as the new and younger face of the French radical right but she has been perceived as a strategic person—a leader who has prodigiously accelerated the de-demonization of the FN's image and has been very careful to avoid controversial statements. For instance—unlike her father, who has faced many lawsuits—she has not been found guilty of Holocaust denial or anti-Semitism in the courts (Machuret 2012: 11). Aware that anti-Jewish rhetoric will be costly at the electoral level, she has always refrained from jokes on such subjects (Corbière and Pena-Ruiz 2012: 19).[38] In comparison with her father, she is the embodiment of some *sof LePenism*. She has coined the term *Marinism* to emphasize her break with the party's hardline tradition. When she describes the party, she prefers to define her political line as national right, popular and social, thus avoiding use of the word "extreme" (Bornschier 2012). In this sense, the term *Marinism* refers not just to this new direction but also serves to distance her from her father's controversial leadership style.

Although Marine Le Pen has tried to portray a softer image of the FN externally, internally she has used the same strategies as her father did. First, the family remains the nucleus of the FN's political leadership. Marine Le Pen's companion,

---

[38]However, she does not refrain completely from hate speech. In December 2010, she spoke at a political rally in Lyon and compared Muslims praying on public streets to "the German occupation of France in World War II". She stated, "For those who like to speak about the Second World War, here we can talk about occupation ... certainly there are no tanks, there are no soldiers, but it weighs heavily on local people". Following this incident, she temporarily lost her European parliamentary immunity and was fined (Euroactiv 2014). However, she was acquitted in court in 2015. According to the judge, her remarks fell under the rubric of freedom of expression (*Le Monde* 2015).

4.1 Leadership: Jean-Marie Le Pen Versus Marine Le Pen

Louis Aliot, is vice-president of the FN; her brother-in-law, Philippe Oliver, is one of her most influential advisors; and her sister, Yann, is a discreet and omnipresent advisor (Monnot and Mestre 2011: 18). In addition, a third generation of Le Pens have recently started to make their appearance on the political stage. Most prominent among them is Marion Maréchal Le Pen. She is the youngest deputy in the French National Assembly and at the forefront of the party's leadership; among others, she led the FN's list in the southern region of Alps, Provence and Cote d'Azur for the regional elections in late 2015 and earned the best result of all FN top list candidates in any region (her list obtained 40.55 % of the vote in the first round and 45.22 % in the second round) (*Ministère de l'Intérieur* 2015b). The name Le Pen helped in the regional elections, but even more in the 2012 general election campaign, when she was less well-known than she is now: she took great advantage of her family name to secure her election to the French National Assembly (Lebourg and Beauregard 2012: 385).

Second, Marine Le Pen governs the FN with the same iron fist as did her father. In fact, from the onset of her presidency, she has been very successful in affirming her authority within the party. As early as April 2011, only 3 months after her election as the new FN president, she expelled 10 supporters of her rival, Bruno Gollnisch. Officially, she justified their expulsion by their radical positions, which did not correspond to the official party line, but unofficially it is probably also safe to argue that an additional target of this purge was *L'Oeuvre Française*, an extremist rightest group that was not favourable to her election to the FN's presidency. This group was perceived by Le Pen and her supporters as a real threat—as a group that was aiming to take control of the party (Monnot and Mestre 2011: 142–143). Since then, party members who either pose a threat to Le Pen or, more frequently, have not followed the new rhetorical line of relative moderation have been expelled.

Rather paradoxically, the only real internal threat to Marine Le Pen's leadership has been her father. Because the idea of succession has been very difficult for him to bear, if not impossible to conceive, Jean-Marie Le Pen has repeatedly questioned Marine Le Pen's leadership style and the new ideology of *Marinisme* (Cohen and Péan 2012: 473). For example, he has repeatedly criticized her softness and returned to his anti-Semitic jokes. Most obviously, as a guest on the French radio channel Europe 1 on April 2, 2015, he reaffirmed his statement about the gas chamber as a "detail" of Second World War history (Pasteau 2015). However, Marine Le Pen did not allow her father to challenge her leadership this way. When he continued to present her as a weak leader and who is directly under the influence of her party management (formed of Louis Aliot and Florian Philippot), she did not hesitate to engage in procedures to have him expelled from the party (*La Libération* 2015).

On August 20, 2015, Jean-Marie Le Pen was suspended from the FN, although he retained his position as the party's honorary president. The decision was made by majority vote of the *Bureau Exécutif* (L'Express 2015). Even though he attacked his daughter aggressively after his expulsion, among other things calling her a traitor, the family feud did not hurt the FN or Marine Le Pen.[39] Despite uneasiness among some members, there has been no sign of decline in FN membership. Among the general public, this move to marginalize her father has brought Marine Le Pen more rather than less sympathy, as approximately 70 % of the French electorate supported the expulsion of Jean-Marie Le Pen from the party (Huffington Post 2015).

Third, and even more than her father, Marine Le Pen has created a personality cult around her name. Using the strategy of populism, she presents herself as a new type of leader (see also Chap. 3), one who is pure and honest and who takes the concerns and sorrows of common people seriously. She is the personification of the party: it is her name, rather than the party name, that appears in party programmes and documents and on the Internet platform. When she gives a speech, it is as if a pop star is appearing on stage. To close the distance with voters, supporters, and members, she wants them to refer to her as Marine, portraying the image that she is one of them. FN members and candidates follow this personality cult. For example, several FN candidates in the 2014 local elections used pictures of Marine Le Pen instead of pictures of themselves in their campaign literature (Vivas and Vivas 2014: 91).

4.2 The Party Elites Under Jean-Marie Le Pen and Marine Le Pen

As noted, the family has always been an important criterion in the attribution of party responsibilities and offices under both Jean-Marie Le Pen and Marine Le Pen. Yet, a national party cannot be run by a family alone; other individuals are necessary for a party to function. The composition of the FN elites differs somewhat from Jean-Marie Le Pen to Marine Le Pen. The former picked individuals with a decidedly far-right-wing background and only some technocrats in the 1980s and 1990s, whereas the latter has so far chosen people with whom she has worked before, individuals, who were strong in *Génération Le Pen*. She has also realized that she needs individuals with the necessary organizational skills to run the party.

4.2.1 Jean-Marie Le Pen

During Jean-Marie Le Pen's presidency, the majority of influential positions within the FN hierarchy was occupied by individuals with a rather hardline ideology, with whom Jean-Marie Le Pen shared some personal experience, friendship, or personal affinity. Among those with whom he had personal experience were long-term executive member and Vice-president Bruno Gollnisch, who was the prototype of

---

[39] Among other things, Jean-Marie Le Pen commented that he was "deeply shocked, hurt, and the victim of a political witch-hunt" and would not support his daughter in the 2017 presidential election (New York Times 2015).

4.2 The Party Elites Under Jean-Marie Le Pen and Marine Le Pen   49

a faithful follower. Ideologically close to Le Pen, Gollnisch has always supported him, and in compensation he has occupied influential posts in the party for decades. It is worth noting that Gollnisch has remained faithful to Jean-Marie Le Pen even though Le Pen supported Marine Le Pen in the internal competition for his successor (Gollnisch 2015). Gollnisch has also supported Jean-Marie Le Pen in his internal struggles with Marine Le Pen. He was one of few influential FN members who publicly condemned Jean-Marie Le Pen's expulsion from the party.

Long-time Executive Committee member Alain Jamet is typical of an FN member whose career resembles Jean-Marie Le Pen's. Jamet was very active alongside Le Pen in the Tixier-Vignancour Committees, joined the FN in 1972 along with Le Pen, and shared his experience as a former combatant in Algeria (Le Monde 2014c). Finally, Christine Arnautu is the perfect example of a family friend who has made a career in the FN. A personal friend of Le Pen's (he is the godparent of one of her children), Arnautu has accessed the highest positions within the FN (among others, she has been a long-term vice president of the party and deputy to the European Parliament) (Arnautu 2015).

Despite his tendency to nominate individuals with whom he had a personal affinity to high inner-party offices, Jean-Marie Le Pen also made some strategic appointments, albeit only in the 1980s and 1990s. In the 1980s, when the FN started to break with his political marginality, he began to recruit new cadres. For example, in the early 1980s, Jean-Marie Le Chevallier, a former chief of staff of a French state secretary, became Jean-Marie Le Pen's chief of staff and joined the Bureau Politique, the FN's politburo (Igounet 2014: 145). In 1986, to reap the most benefits from the proportional electoral system set up by the *François Mitterrand's* leftist government for the legislative elections of that year, Le Pen worked hard to present a more respectable image of his party. In fact, his striving to become more mainstream in the eyes of the voters was never more pronounced than in that year. He tried to attract candidates from social elites and the establishment; many of these recruits were newcomers, even non-members. Le Pen hoped that their technical skills would show that the FN's parliamentary group had some real political expertise (Albertini and Doucet 2013: 126). In addition, the FN candidates ran under the *Rassemblement National* label during that election instead of using the party's name.

It was also in 1986 that Bruno Mégret, a technocrat and experienced politician from the moderate right with much experience running campaigns, joined the party. Thanks to his organizational skills, he moved up in the organization in no time. In 1987, he became campaign manager; shortly thereafter, he occupied the key position of "*Délégué General*" (general delegate), which gave him a great deal of influence within the party structure. Thus, only 2 years after taking out party membership, he was seen as the FN's number two, a position he occupied for nearly 10 years (Lebourg and Beauregard 2012). Despite his expulsion in 1998, Mégret has been very influential in shaping the FN. He was the first to try to change the party's image permanently and not just for one election, as Jean-Marie Le Pen did in 1986. He wanted the FN to look like a government party. His ideological conception was not embedded in the traditional right. Rather, he was one of the first representatives of the new right, the ideological current that is now dominant in the FN. Although Marine Le Pen is credited for the party's deradicalizaton, it was Mégret who began this trend (Albertini and Doucet 2013). In this sense, Marine Le Pen is mimicking strategies that Mégret introduced more than 15 years ago.

However, the FN at the time was not ready for this ideological innovation. In many ways, Mégret was an anomaly within the FN, presenting a profile that was very different from those of the FN's original elites. He was the prototype of the French establishment that the FN used to denounce. He graduated as an engineer from the Polytechnique and had a degree from the American elite school the University of California, Berkeley (Lebourg and Beauregard 2012: 143). During Jean-Marie Le Pen's presidency, Mégret's conception of the party was too progressive to prevail. He clashed with Jean-Marie Le Pen because the latter did not want an updating of the FN's message. Furthermore, Le Pen saw in Mégret a serious challenge to his absolute leadership and power. Consequently, the FN leader expelled him from the party and replaced him with more "extreme" figures as the party's number 2 (first Jack Lang and then Bruno Gollnisch). After the Mégret episode, there were no more attempts by Jean-Marie Le Pen to renew the party's image. Instead, appointments remained faithful to the FN's traditional line.

4.2.2 Marine Le Pen

Since 2011, when Marine Le Pen became the FN's new president, the composition of the party's elites (e.g. the executive bureau) has somewhat changed. In particular, Marine Le Pen has replaced the old elites (e.g. Bruno Gollnisch and Alain Jamet), with individuals of her own age, catapulting a new generation of FN elites to the fore. This new elite (e.g. Luis Aliot, Bruno Bilde, and Steeve Brios) is composed mainly of people in their forties who have always been close to Marine Le Pen, both personally and ideologically. In fact, the majority of the new leadership is composed of former members of *Génération Le Pen*, a parallel FN organization that she created in 2002 to give the FN a more dynamic, younger, and less radical image (Igounet 2014: 371–372). Representatives of this group account for more than half of the new leadership; many of them made their careers alongside Marine Le Pen, first in the FN youth organization FNJ and then in *Génération Le Pen* (Monnot and Mestre 2011: 24).

Because of their common background, the members of this new elite are also ideologically more coherent than was the old elite; they stem from the 1968 generation and were politically socialized in the Mitterrand years. In contrast to the FN founders, they were not directly affected by the historical periods of the Second World War and French Algeria and by the issues and divisions associated with these two periods (Perrineau 2014: 71–72). An interesting side note is that many key people in this new generation of influential FN members are former Mégret supporters. They left the FN in winter 1998–1999, after he seceded from the party. However, when they realized that Mégret's new party was not taking off either in elections or in membership numbers, some of these *félons* (traitors, as Jean-Marie Le Pen called them) returned to the FN in the early 2000s. This was the case for Steeve Briois and Bruno Bidle, who became, respectively, secretary general of the FN and Marine Le Pen's chief of staff after her election to the party presidency in January 2011 (Crépon 2012: 83).

Like her father, who ran the party in the 1980s and 1990s with Mégret's help, Marine Le Pen has a technocrat as general manager of the party, Florian Philippot (Machuret 2012: 184). Similar to Mégret, Philippot is a typical representative of the French elites. He graduated from the Ecole Nationale d'Administration, which, like the Polytechnique, has many graduates from the French political and state elites. He seems to play the same role that Mégret played under Jean-Marie Le Pen's leadership. He represents the intercultural face of the FN, and he coordinates and runs the party (Lebourg and Beauregard 2012: 366). The presence of Philippot in the tiny circle of influence around Marine Le Pen is the best example of the new soft image that she wants to give to her party, but it is also the source of internal tensions, especially from FN hardliners. For a party that historically has been homophobic, the presence of homosexual people such as Philippot around the new president raises political questions. Rather unsurprisingly, internal opposition mainly comes from Jean-Marie Le Pen and his followers. It is more than ironic that the person who has engaged in the most favouritism in the party's history is now questioning the construction of a "gay lobby" within the FN, in which executives' seats are allocated to friends.

When it comes to the presentation of the FN in elections, Marine Le Pen again reproduces a strategy that Jean-Marie Le Pen employed in the 1986 elections. Led by her ambition to create a governing party, she has tried to attract new faces—individuals from outside the party—to her electoral list. Similar to her father's labelling the FN list *Rassemblement National* in 1986, she coined the name *Rassemblement Bleu Marine* for her list (Igounet 2014: 427). This opening up of electoral space bore some fruit: Gilbert Collard, a well-known French lawyer, was elected as one of the three FN deputies in the 2012 legislative election (Lebourg and Beauregard 2012: 384).

In sum, the leadership style has changed in form, but not in substance, from Jean-Marie Le Pen to Marine Le Pen. Marine Le Pen wants to give the FN a new outlook, a softer image, even though the FN's fundamental positions remain unchanged (Dézé 2015). To do this, she uses the same three strategies that her father has used in the 1980s and early 1990s: having professional staff and a general manager able to organize the party (although he is not liked by everyone in the party, Florian Philippot fulfils this criterion); using inclusive lists in elections that include non-FN members to portray some openness; and the creation of a personality cult around her name. Yet these changes should not hide the fact that Marine Le Pen has so far ruled the FN with the same iron fist as did her father. She is the absolute leader of the FN, surrounded by her faithful, and continues to favour family members in the allocation of inner-party responsibilities. All these features make the party under Marine Le Pen not that different after all from the party under Jean-Marie Le Pen.

4.3 The FN's Relationship with the Media Under Jean-Marie Le Pen and Marine Le Pen

When discussing the two leaders' relationship with the media, two things come to the fore. First, the FN's electoral success has always been closely linked to the party's representation in the media. Second, of all of their leadership characteristics, Jean-Marie Le Pen and Marine Le Pen probably differ the most in their relationship with the media. Even though the FN has always had a love–hate relationship with the media, each FN president had a different conception of how to use it. Particularly under Jean-Marie Le Pen, the notion of a conspiracy theory was one of the main pillars in the FN ideology; he repeatedly insisted that the media conspire with political elites to destabilize the FN (Quinn 2000: 112). His strategy was characterized by two elements: the portrayal of the FN as a victim of media propaganda that has been treated unfairly by the media conglomerate and the use of the media as an outlet to circulate his provocations. In contrast, since taking the reins of the party, Marine Le Pen has tried to normalize the relationship that she and the party have with the media. In fact, unlike during her father's reign, the media are no longer a main target in the FN's anti-elite discourse and propositions.

4.3.1 Jean-Marie Le Pen

For the first 10 years of the party's existence, the FN was literally absent from the media; neither the president nor representatives were ever invited to radio or television programmes. Hence, the political marginality and electoral failures between 1972 and 1982, which are commonly labelled as *la traversée du desert* (the crossing of the desert) (Cohen and Péan 2012), were in part linked to a complete lack of accessibility to mainstream media outlets, all of which were at the time all public. The political class did not want to provide the radical right with a platform for disseminating its message despite the fact that under the Fifth Republic access to the media is guaranteed by law to all political parties that are not represented in the parliament. Many excuses were found to deny Jean-Marie Le Pen and his party media exposure. One example of this media isolation was the French parliamentary elections of 1978. Under the pretext that its application had not been presented within the official deadline, the FN was denied access to all radio and television electoral propaganda programmes (Lorien et al. 1985: 145).

However, things began to change in the early 1980s. The first leftist government in the Fifth Republic thought that it would be a strategically beneficial move to grant Le Pen some media time. In fact, it was through the personal intervention of the then sitting president, *François Mitterrand*, that Le Pen gained his first television appearance. Wishing to weaken the moderate right rather than to ensure the presence in the public media of all political forces in France, Mitterrand asked his Communication's Minister to intervene with top management at the public

4.3 The FN's Relationship with the Media Under Jean-Marie Le Pen and Marine Le Pen

television network to have Jean-Marie Le Pen appear on a major TV channel (Perrineau 2014: 20–21).[40] On June 29, 1982, Jean-Marie Le Pen made his first appearance on the late newscast on TF1. For Le Pen, it was a golden opportunity and a first step towards media access.

Given his charisma and good oratorical skills, Jean-Marie Le Pen's first appearance was successful and helped him break the glass ceiling of media exclusion. In the months and years to come, he became a regular guest on news programmes, debates, and other television shows. Despite the fact that the motivations for these invitations were negative—the public media tried to portray him as adhering to a racist or fascist ideology (Le Bohec 2005: 15)—his renewed media presence allowed him to gain visibility and public attention. In fact, it did not take long for him to become a media favourite. In particular, after the FN gained its first-ever significant electoral result in the small town of Dreux, with 16.7 % of the votes in the 1983 municipal election, the media started to be intrigued by the FN. In the words of Cohen and *Péan* (2012: 206), the "thunder of Dreux" triggered a public and media debate about the FN, its programme, and its leader, and the hype enabled Le Pen to become a regular on major outlets. Most importantly, the partial electoral success in Dreux triggered an invitation to *L'heure de vérité*, the most-watched political TV show at the time.

On February 14, 1984, *L'heure de vérité* won the ratings race for its time slot, with 54 % of the TV audience watching the interview with Jean-Marie Le Pen. Le Pen benefited in two ways from this major TV appearance. First, it gave him the opportunity to convey to the French public that "Le Pen says aloud what all the others think quietly" (Marcilly and Le Pen 1984: 201). Second, the way the interview was conducted played in Le Pen's favour. The journalists on stage, divided over his presence, showed aggressiveness towards the man whom they considered to be a provocateur and a xenophobe (Igounet 2014: 147). Facing many (personal) attacks, Le Pen remained calm and well-behaved, portraying him as a *bon client* facing down the elites' unfounded attacks (Le Bohec 2005: 26).

Within a week of his television appearance, voting intentions for Le Pen rose from 3.5 % to 7 %, paving the way for the party's first national success in the 1984 European Elections, in which the FN won slightly over 10 % of the vote (Bresson and Lionet 1994: 409). Le Pen had won his bet. After a decade of media marginality, he finally could make good use of his charisma and talent as a good communicator in the main media outlets. The renewed media access was central to the FN's assent and preceded the party's electoral expansion. Le Pen was given credence by benevolent national and local media outlets that either did not actively seek to delegitimize the FN or, if they tried to do so, as on *L'heure de verité*, failed miserably (Copsey 1997: 108).

---

[40]In fact, according to Albertini and Doucet (2013), by opening up the media path and introducing the PR system into parliamentary elections in 1986, among other things, Mitterrand deliberately favoured the FN. However, this was probably a successful move for Mitterrand because it deflected the public dissatisfaction with his own party and policies and weakened the moderate right.

However, despite the fact that Jean-Marie Le Pen became a media favourite—between 1983 and 1995 he was a guest on *L'heure de vérité* seven times, more than any other French politician—his media relations remained controversial, and this was deliberate on his part. His strategy was based on two pillars: first, despite the fact that French media helped the FN to enter mainstream politics in terms of both credibility and exposure, and despite the fact that quantitatively the FN, compared to its size, has been over- rather than underrepresented in the media since the 1980s, Le Pen tended to portray himself as a victim of a media boycott (Quinn 2000: 116–117). For example, he repeatedly complained that the media does not talk enough about his party or, if it does talk about it, portrays the party as racist, xenophobic, or fascist—all labels that, according to him, are unfounded (Mathias 2007: 39).

Second, Jean-Marie Le Pen has always used the media as an outlet for circulating his polemical declarations. In particular, in important political times, he has tried to focus media attention on himself, using whatever means necessary to do so. For him the winning formula has always been quite simple, but very efficient: "Whatever they say about the FN, good or bad things, what is important is that they talk about it" (quoted in Le Bohec 2005: 25). Hence, media coverage of Jean-Marie Le Pen has been essentially negative. In headlines and editorials, journalists have tended to denounce his provocations, and, despite inviting him to appear on many occasions, have remained rather hostile to him.

It is true that Jean-Marie Le Pen has faced media attacks for decades. However, to a certain degree, he has always been able to counter this negative image by presenting himself as a common-sense figure who is reviled by the establishment for saying what everybody knows (Mathias 2007: 232). In fact, many of what have been presented by the media as Le Pen's *gaffes* were probably not so much mistakes, but carefully prepared events directed towards his electoral base (Bell 1994: 231). This is even more likely given that some FN members and supporters have always been fascinated by his charisma and care less about the negative image inflicted on him by the media than about the candid discourse. Hence, it is unclear if and to what degree the negative reporting in the media, which Le Pen has to large degree shaped himself, has helped or hurt him politically (Mathias 2007: 40). Yet, in this debate is something Jean-Marie Le Pen probably forgot, but we should not forget: that it was the media that helped to bring him and the party to the political forefront (Jouve and Magoudi 1988: 174).

4.3.2 Marine Le Pen

Marine Le Pen's media strategy is a reversal of her father's. Since she has taken the presidency of the party, she has devoted much attention to normalizing the FN's image in the media. It has been her goal to nullify the party's old image as one that is xenophobic, racist, and anti-Semitic—all attributes that were associated with her father's leadership. Rather than cultivating this old image, she aims to present the

FN as a government party able to take power (Igounet 2014: 19). Her anti-elitist programme and rhetoric exempts the media. Her *dédiabolisation* strategy strongly targets the media; she intends to build a "soft respectable image of the party", first in the media and then among the general public (Monnot and Mestre 2011: 15). In particular, and despite the continued presence of more hard-core elements within the party, she aims to reassure voters and potential electors that the FN is a serious party that adheres to republican values (albeit with a nationalistic twist) and is determined and competent enough to take power.

Marine Le Pen had attempted to break with her father's controversial image and relationship with the media long before she became the FN leader. In fact, the deradicalization process had started as early as 2002 (Machuret 2012), when she made her first improvised but noticeable media appearances, such as the one on May 22, 2002, when she successfully debated Jean-Luc Mélenchon, an experienced and well-known French politician from the radical left (Monnot and Mestre 2011: 14). More media performances followed; in all of them Marine Le Pen appeared strong. In 2007, she also became the party's media spokesperson, when she was appointed vice-president of the FN in charge of training, propaganda, and information (Igounet 2014: 408).

Marine Le Pen performed very well as the FN's media liaison. For press, radio, and television outlets, she quickly became a new favourite and aggressive spokesperson pushing the FN's position without her father's slips (Machuret 2012: 80). Like her father, she has good communicational skills, but she has a different rhetorical style and does not use provocative words and phrases that cause media scandals (Corbiere and Pena-Ruiz 2012: 18). According to Crépon (2012: 72), "Her ease on the television screen, her sense of repartee in presence of other politicians, her ability to attract attention, and probably also the fact that she is a Le Pen made the media machine very excited about her".

Marine Le Pen's good media relations strongly benefited her in the internal competition for the FN presidency in 2010 and 2011. On December 9, 2010, she was the guest on the main political TV show broadcast by France 2, *À Vous de Juger* (For You to Judge). Her charisma, her ease in answering questions, and the softer image she portrayed of the FN were convincing (Monnot and Mestre 2011: 14). Within only 24 hours of her appearance, the FN's ranks swelled by 5000 new members (Le Goff 2011). The same year, the centre-right newspaper *Le Figaro* took a favourable position towards her in the battle with Bruno Gollnisch for the FN presidency. In fact, in the view of several scholars (Cohen and Péan 2012: 493; Monnot and Mestre 2011: 14), her media performances were instrumental in shaping a positive image of her.

Since taking over the FN leadership, Marine Le Pen has further cultivated her relations with the media. For 10 years, and on TV show after TV show, she has built her personal media image, which is different from her father's image. She does not suffer from any media stigma. On the contrary, the media accept her as a modern woman, a representative of a new generation of party leaders (Monnot and Mestre 2011: 19). If it were not for the continued provocations of Jean-Marie Le Pen and some local and regional FN leaders, it would seem that she has convinced the media with her deradicalization strategy. Certainly she has gone a long way towards winning the media image battle. She has definitely managed to make her party less disturbing to public opinion (half of the French population perceive the party as a party like others now [Crépon 2012: 76]). However, transforming the FN's image from a right-wing fringe party to a main contender in French politics takes time and continued effort. Marine Le Pen knows that this transformation can be successful only with the help of the media; therefore, she continues to rely heavily on them (Machuret 2012: 63).

4.4 The Leadership Styles of Jean-Marie and of Marine Le Pen: A Synopsis

In this chapter, I have shown that there are many commonalities between Jean-Marie Le Pen and Marine Le Pen. Both leaders have personified the FN, created a personality cult around their name, governed the party with an iron fist, favoured the appointment of family members to important internal offices, and appointed their personal friends or followers to important inner-party positions. However, the two leaders have differed in their communication strategies and their relationship with the media. Except for during the mid-1980s, Jean-Marie Le Pen has never really tried to soften the party's image. Throughout his career, he has remained faithful to a traditional radical or extreme-right-wing ideology, including latent anti-Semitism and a complete rejection of the French establishment. His media provocations were deliberate and aimed to stir controversy. In contrast, using the same strategies as Bruno Mégret has done in the 1980s and 1990s, Marine Le Pen has tried to give the party a softer image. Among others, she has used acceptable language, rarely has employed any slips, and, most importantly, she has tried to work with the media rather than against it.

Chapter 5
The FN Membership Under Jean-Marie Le Pen and Marine Le Pen

Marine Le Pen's ascension to the presidency of the FN in November 2011 has been a blessing for the radical right-wing party in terms of membership. She has made the party more popular than it ever was before. In under 4 years (2011 to 2014), FN membership nearly quadrupled. In January 2011, several months before Marine Le Pen was elected president, the party had somewhat over 22,000 members; its membership nearly doubled in the 3 months after the election of the new leader, to 40,000, in February 2012. In 3 months, the party attracted nearly 20,000 members; this means that, on average, more than 200 members joined the party daily in the first half of 2011. Between then and the end of 2014, the number of members again doubled. As of December 2014, the FN had approximately 83,000 dues-paying members, making it the third-largest party in France in terms of its membership (see Figs. 5.1 and 5.2). Who are these members? Do they still fit the profile of traditional right-wing activists, or has the profile changed with this massive influx of newcomers? Is the membership under Marine Le Pen less radical and more mainstream than were the majority of members under Jean-Marie Le Pen?

These are the questions that I aim to answer in this chapter. To do so, I use a mixture of secondary and primary sources. The secondary sources describe the FN membership under Jean-Marie Le Pen. I collected the primary sources (mainly interview data) during a 7-month field research stay in France in 2013. Juxtaposing the secondary literature to my primary findings, I systematically compare the old membership under Jean-Marie Le Pen to the new membership under Marine Le Pen across various categories, such as the political socialization of the members, the members' beliefs and their ideology, and their motives for engagement. However, before doing so, Figs. 5.1 and 5.2 briefly present the interview data that serves as the basis for analysis of the current FN members.

Fig. 5.1 FN membership, 2011–2014. Source: Le Figaro (2014)

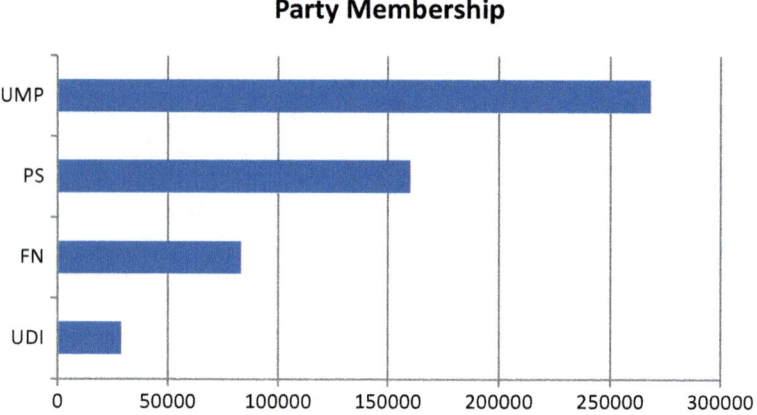

Fig. 5.2 Membership in France's main parties. Source: Le Figaro (2014)

5.1 Method and Interview Sample

To learn more about FN members, I engaged in a 7-month field research project in France between January and July 2013. My main goal was to get to know the FN movement and, in particular, its members from the inside. I visited more than 15 departmental chapters of the FN in all parts of France, participated in and observed their activities, and formally interviewed 44 FN members. To get access to the members, I normally contacted the departmental secretary and asked if he or she would be willing to talk to me and to distribute my request for interviewees on the departmental e-mail list servers. I made it clear from the onset that I was not visiting various FN chapters to judge the activists, betray them, or get inside information.

5.1 Method and Interview Sample

Rather, it was my goal to understand the members of the FN, their political socialization, goals, values and ideologies, and trajectory in the organization.

The reactions of the departmental secretaries were generally positive, but varied from individual to individual. Some asked me to speak to them by phone; others invited me to an informal meeting. A third group agreed to an interview right away. In three or four cases, my message was also distributed on the departmental list server immediately. Sometimes, my initial contact person was a little wary and somewhat hesitant about my intentions.[41] However, once I established initial contact and explained the rationale for and goals of my study to the contact person and the broader membership, communication with various FN chapters and members went quite smoothly. After an initial interview or contact, my interlocutors were frequently very helpful, introduced me to more members, and tried to help me in my research.[42] Some FN departmental secretaries also actively helped me in my attempts to diversify my sample and assisted with recruiting the type of activist that I needed the most at any given moment. For example, if, within one departmental chapter, I had talked to two or three people who were older and had been party members for over 20 or 25 years, I asked departmental secretaries with whom I had established good rapport if they knew of any younger members who had just joined and might be willing to talk to me. Most of the time, the interview process was iterative; it frequently happened that I visited the same chapter several times for interviews. Whenever possible, I also tried to attend some of the official events organized by the local or regional FN chapters.[43]

The mixture of snowball and purposeful sampling allowed me to gain a relatively balanced sample of FN activists.[44] Since the focus of this research was on grass-roots activists, I did not include any staff or professional employees in my sample of interviewees but only individuals who chose to become unpaid activists in the movement. In terms of demographics and characteristics of the members, I talked to a diverse sample of people. Young, middle-aged, and elderly members, men and women, strongly engaged and weakly engaged activists, and activists who only pay their membership dues were all in my sample.[45] In total, 40 individuals

---

[41] Some of the departmental secretaries in the Paris region were a little wary because a journalist had infiltrated a local chapter less than one year before I conducted my field research. She wrote a book about her experience in the FN, which made some FN members angry.

[42] I also asked the departmental secretaries about the composition of local FN members to obtain some more general information on the party's membership.

[43] The FN chapters were very keen to invite me to official events such as speaker series and information stands aiming to portray an "authentic" image of the party.

[44] Geographically, I covered various parts of France. I visited local areas where the FN has been very strong both in terms of electoral performance and in terms of membership (such as Rhône Alps and Lorraine), as well as chapters in regions where the FN is electorally weak and has relatively low membership (such as Pays de Loire and Brittany).

[45] In terms of age, I interviewed individuals between 19 and 69. In terms of engagement level, I talked to activists who are members on paper and pay their dues but are otherwise not active and to very engaged individuals who spend more than 30 hours per week working for their cause.

were FN members and 4 interviewees were engaged primarily in the FN youth organization, FNJ. In the terms of length of membership, I interviewed individuals who had been members for over 25 or 30 years and people who had joined the organization weeks or months before the interview. About one-half of the interviewees had some kind of function within the movement (e.g. they served on the regional board or as the party's local representative or contact person); the other half were simply activists with no official position. The activists in my sample also come from different backgrounds. For example, I talked to former Algerian settlers, former UDF/ UMP members, traditional Catholics, and previously politically uninvolved citizens.

The interviews took place in mainly three types of locations—individuals' homes, the FN regional headquarters, or a restaurant or bar. Most of the interviews had a formal and an informal component. The formal component was the actual interview, for which I used an interview guide including questions on the members' political socialization, their motivation for engagement, their values and beliefs, and their trajectory within the organization. In an open conversational format, I tried to reconstruct the members' political career, from the time when they became interested in politics to the day of the interview (Aminzade 1993: 108). In most cases, we conversed about an individual's activist career in chronological order, but in some cases the activist explained his or her political socialization, engagement, and goals and motivations in a non linear fashion.

The formal component of the interview lasted between 30 minutes and more than 3 hours, with a median interview time of slightly over an hour. After the interview, I frequently continued to chat informally with the members over a drink, coffee, or dinner. For example, it happened frequently when I was invited to somebody's home that they asked me to stay for coffee or a meal. When I met the members at a bar or restaurant, we often ordered some food after the interview. When I conducted interviews in the party's local or regional office or the FN's regular meeting location, my interviewee or the departmental secretary often introduced me to other members, who did not necessarily want to do any official interview but were very keen to get to know me. During these unofficial conversations, I heard a good deal of gossip about the activists' careers and got to hear some anecdotes from their activist lives. I recorded the official part of any interview and, whenever the activists allowed me to do so, I tried to take notes during these informal conversations. Right after the interview, I tried to complete these notes to the best of my ability.[46]

---

[46]The interactions, experiences, and contacts that I had with many of the FN members were quite pleasant. For the most part, they respected that I had different political views, opinions, and goals and did not try to convince me that their world view is superior to mine. I tried to be very open about my own political beliefs, and almost to a person the FN activists appreciated this frankness. In fact, except for two encounters, in which I was insulted because I acknowledged supporting gay marriage and voiced my support for the European Union, respectively, the FN members were very courteous and respectful towards me and my beliefs and values.

5.1 Method and Interview Sample

Like most researchers conducting in-depth semi-structured interviews, I had to tackle two caveats: the representativeness of my sample and the possibility that FN activists were communicating a softer, more respectable version of their beliefs to me. Pertaining to the first issue, I am fully aware that my sample is not fully representative. Nevertheless, I maintain that I assembled a fairly diversified pool of interviews that fairly accurately reflects the FN members' political socialization, values, beliefs, and goals. First, as noted above, I talked to various types of members, with various types of activist experiences, various political backgrounds, and various degrees of commitment to the movement. Second, I conducted more interviews than many qualitative methods' texts propose (Adler and Adler 1987; Guest et al. 2006). Third, during every interview, I also tried to add one or two questions about the other members in the movement to have some comparative element. Fourth, and most importantly, I found that I reached some kind of saturation at the end of the interview period. In particular, there was consistency in the members' values and belief system regardless of their political socialization, their personal and professional backgrounds, and their length of membership.

Second, there is always the possibility that interviewees communicate an acceptable and softer version of their beliefs. In my case, this could apply rather easily, because I was dealing with members of a party at one extreme of the political spectrum. Several indications led me to reject this hypothesis. First, FN members are convinced that their world view represents the truth; they want to persuade others that their point of view is correct. Rather than hiding their world views, which sometimes have a touch of racism or include strong anti-establishment opinions, they want to spread their vision of the world. They therefore have some inherent interest in my writing about their ideology and value system. Second, some of the interviewees were passionate and emotional in their opinions; they sometimes used strong words and different intonations to make their voice heard. Third, many members appreciated the open approach that I employed when I introduced myself. They trusted me and were flattered that I had come from a foreign country to learn more about them. In the words of one interviewee, "I appreciate that somebody neutral, who is not part of the French corrupt elites, comes and speaks to us" (Interview 13). Finally, for the most part, I was speaking with rank and file members. Two out of three of my conversation partners had never given any informal or formal interview before they talked to me, and they do not know how the FN is characterized in academia and what has been written about them. They thus have no reason to hide any darker side of their beliefs.

Using the same order that I tried to follow in each interview, I discuss the FN members' socio-economic background, their political socialization, their values (both political and personal), their motivation for engagement and commitment, and their trajectory as party activists below. For each of these four dimensions, I try to juxtapose my findings with the traditional secondary literature on right-wing extremists in France and elsewhere. This enables me to detect some commonalities and differences between activists under Jean-Marie Le Pen and those under Marine Le Pen.

5.2 Activists Under Jean-Marie Le Pen and Marine Le Pen

5.2.1 Activists' Socio-Economic Background

Traditionally, right-wing activists in France (and elsewhere) have been described as marginalized people with low income and little education, who live isolated from the rest of the population and adhere to traditional gender roles (Falter 1983; Payne Stanely 1996). To support this view, Bizeul (2003) describes the FN membership in the late 1990s and early 2000s as a "community of victims" (19)—outcasts who find refuge within the party and consequently possess a strong sense of solidarity among its members (65). In terms of socio-economic background, he finds that together, the working class and the unemployed make up the majority of the membership, representing 30 % and 38 % of members, respectively. Adding some gendered analysis, Birenbaum (1992) describes the FN members as an "old boys' club" that reinforces the traditional gender roles of men and women in politics. In fact, according to the author, 82 % of FN members in the late 1980s were men and only 18 % were women (many of whom were also uninvolved).

Today, this restrictive description of FN activists no longer seems to apply. The interviewees I talked to come from different backgrounds and a wide variety of organizations. For example, I talked to individuals of all levels of educational achievement, from middle school to doctorate. In particular, compared to earlier times, it seems that more and more activists have a university education. Professionally, my interview partners were lawyers, business people, students, retirees, police officers, real estate agents, salespeople, nurses, and doctors. Furthermore, and despite a degree of stigmatization that many FN members still face, the activists do not see themselves as social outcasts. Rather, they aim to engage with the mainstream population and institutions to take advantage of political opportunities.

5.2.2 Activists' Political Socialization

The Authoritarian Personality by Adorno et al. (1950) is the classical reference on the right-wing activists' political socialization. According to these authors, extremism is "a syndrome of authoritarian attitudes, formed during childhood by dominating parents" (Adorno et al. 1950: 6). Subsequent studies, focusing on radical activists in France and elsewhere, concur with Adorno's et al. assessment. For example, von Mering and McCarty (2013) argue that the political socialization of radical right-wing activists is rooted in the family, the environment in which individuals develop their personality and identity based on the traditions and culture in which they grow up. In their view, the recruitment of most radical right activists tends to follow a trajectory of continuity rather than one of conversion or compliance. Introducing what they call the legacy effects theory, Goodwin et al. (2012:

890), too, posit that membership in extreme-right-wing parties is concentrated in families and in areas that have historical ties to right-wing extremism.

The specific literature on the members of the *Front National* supports these findings. For example, Klandermans (2013) reports that the family is the ideal cradle for nurturing the subculture of a radical movement; in his view, this phenomenon applies more strongly the more viable and entrenchedt the extremist movement is in the specific country, with France being the ideal case of this phenomenon. He adds that in France, socialization by the family is the most important mechanism for drawing people into the rank and file of an extremist party. Looking only at members of the *Front National*, both Bizeul (2003) and Crépon (2006) affirm that right-wing extremist credentials tend to be passed on through family lineage. Specifically, according to the authors, around one-third of FN members come from "Gaullist" families and slightly more than one-fifth from families involved in the Tixier-Vignancour committees.

Membership in the FN under Marine Le Pen does not fit this one-dimensional characterization of right-wing activists. The family is no longer the sole or major socialization mechanism drawing people into a radical right-wing milieu, but one of many mechanisms, including political socialization in college, formative experiences during adult life, and gradual attraction to the goals and values of the FN over time. Below, I briefly present some of these socialization mechanisms.

5.2.2.1 Political Socialization Within the Family

Although it is no longer the primary socialization mechanism, about 25 % of my interviewees were socialized by parents who embraced radical right-wing thoughts and ideologies. These individuals have a traditional FN background. They are descendants of former Algerian colonizers, come from a traditional Catholic milieu, and/or have parents that were active in the FN or another radical or extreme-right-wing group. Marc is typical of this first group of activists: raised by nationalist parents, who had been punished because of their collaboration with the Nazi authorities during the Second World War, he started to participate in extreme-right-wing groups at the age of 13 or 14, with the encouragement of his father. The first events he engaged in were the demonstration in favour of the war in Algeria and the May 1968 unrest, in opposition to leftist forces (Interview 15). Simon is another example of family socialization. He stated, "My engagement has a long family tradition; since the war in Vendée in the 1790s, my ancestors have fought on the side of reactionary forces. Out of family loyalty I continue this fight" (Interview 35). As a final example, Stephanie explains the family lineage that has driven her activism as follows:

> My family was a victim of Algerian Independence. I was 17 when I arrived in France from Algeria. France was not the country I hoped to find. From my family, from my readings, and in my dreams I had the image of the eternal and glorious France, and when I came to France in the 1960s, I was disappointed. The country and its people were not as great as I thought. During my studies I became involved in the *Ordre Nouveau* and the Guilt. My engagement

was fiercely anti-communist. It was driven by French patriotism and nationalism. (Interview 24)

5.2.2.2 Political Socialization During High School or College

A second recurring socialization mechanism of FN members was politically formative experiences in high school or university. What is true for some left-wing activists—that they form their political beliefs during their high-school and college years, which constitutes a time of cognitive availability (see Jennings and Niemi 1981; McAdam 1988)—is also true for radical right-wing activists. However, in particular, in high school the mechanisms are different. Whereas students are frequently actively recruited into a left-wing milieu or group, the French radical right is demonized by many teachers and fellow students. However, this demonization can trigger some interest and curiosity among students who are searching for their identity. For example, Claude, whose school and teachers were decidedly anti-FN, asked himself, "Are the people in the FN really fascists and racists, as described by my teachers?" Curious about the real image of FN, he went to an event at the local FN chapter. What he found there convinced him. "The people there were super-friendly, explained their convictions to me, and persuaded me to join the ranks of the FN" (Interview 31).[47]

Others, who might already have a latent predisposition for right-wing ideas, completed their political socialization at the Assas Law School in Paris. A rare example in the French university landscape, Assas University has been a bastion of far-right student politics for decades, with the right-wing student federation Union Droit gaining sizable student representation and membership. Four of my interviewees had their political socialization at this university. François is one of them. Embracing a neo-conservative ideology à la Reagan and Thatcher, he thought that his ideas resonated within student circles there and found the environment conducive to joining a right-wing student organization (Interview 4).

5.2.2.3 Political Socialization During Adulthood

A third group of activists developed their activist credentials later in life, during adulthood. These individuals' political ideologies developed either as a result of

---

[47]Similarly, Maude describes her political socialization as follows: I became politically socialized in 2002, when Jean-Marie Le Pen advanced to the second round in the presidential elections. The college professors asked their students, including me, to go to the street to protest against Le Pen. The whole system of national education was against him. I found this incorrect; he advanced fairly to the second round and no public institution should show this kind of bias. Even worse, the demonstration slogans were F like Fascist and N like Nazi, slogans that had nothing to do with the reality. Because of this bias, I became very interested in the FN and finally joined in 2007 at the age of 19.

5.2 Activists Under Jean-Marie Le Pen and Marine Le Pen

some formative or eye-opening events or as a result of major changes in their lives (see Wolnger et al. 1980). Patrick and Charlene are two examples: they have been shaped by what they refer to as personal landmark experiences. Patrick, a former police officer who worked in the outskirts of Strasbourg, recalls the big mess that immigrants created in their neighbourhoods there. He felt helpless and enraged about what he saw: burglaries, burning cars, drug dealing, and physical violence. Because the mainstream parties did not do anything against this state of anarchy and violence, he turned to the FN, which he feels is the only party tackling the problem. Charlene, who owns a small business outside of Paris, works in an environment of insecurity. She feels exhausted because of drug dealing outside of her shop and destruction of her property. She notes, "I have to show my anger against these fanatics, and the only party that listens to me is the FN" (Interview 9).

Others become open to the ideas and goals of the radical right because of some major shift in their life. As a result of a new job, a divorce, or a change in social class, these members become biographically available and attuned to embracing new ideas. Lucy's example is indicative of this group of people. "After a difficult divorce, I found myself alone after moving to Nancy. I got to know a now fellow FN colleague, who talked to me about the FN. I found his arguments convincing and joined as a simple member" (Interview 25). In a more complex example, Maurice's activism was triggered by several changes in his life. After completing his studies, he switched his social status, started to read various political texts, and personally experienced the negative repercussions of the outsourcing of manual labour at his job as a consultant. His reading of works by Balzac and Dostoyevsky, coupled with his own experience, made him believe in the nation, national cohesion, and national strength. According to Maurice, the only party that adheres to these values is the FN (Interview 19).

5.2.2.4 Radicalization of Beliefs During Adulthood

A fourth group of activists are former supporters of mainstream moderate parties who slowly drifted further right to embrace the positions of the radical right. The majority of people in this group are disgruntled supporters of the moderate right, who joined forces with the FN for various reasons. For instance, four individuals said that they had left what was the RPR because they felt betrayed when Jacques Chirac openly asked his supporters to vote for the socialist candidate, Francois Mitterrand, in the run-off of the 1981 presidential elections.[48] More recently, others have felt betrayed by Nicolas Sarkozy. Some of his former supporters have complained that he used a tough discourse on immigration and security, but was soft when it came to actions. Annick explains her disappointment with Sarkozy as

---

[48]Generally, these members have a very poor opinion of Chirac. As Caroline said, "He first was a humanist, than became a politician along the lines of de Gaulle, but then with time and certainly when in power became radical left" (Interview 16).

follows: "I donated money to the Sarkozy campaign in 2007. He seemed to engage in a tough policy, was charismatic, and made me believe that we would defend our motherland. But after the 5 years of his presidency, I was disappointed, because he did not do anything to defend France. As a president and person he was not extraordinary at all" (Interview 21).

Others blamed Sarkozy for not respecting the sovereignty of the French people. For example, Serge states,

> "I joined the FN in reaction to Sarkozy, whose policy regarding Europe did not sit well with me. Despite the fact that the European treaty was rejected by the people in 2005, he had the same treaty, now called the Lisbon Treaty, ratified in parliament" (Interview 15).

A third type of former supporters of the mainstream right switched allegiance because they became disgruntled with the patronizing and hierarchical climate within the RPR or, later, the UMP. For example, Jessica did not feel that she was taken seriously and respected by the RPR policy apparatus and representatives. She stated,

> Having always believed in individual initiative and individual freedoms, I became an active member of the RPR at the age of 25. However, I soon found out that there is hypocrisy in the ranks of the moderate right. Elected officials think about themselves before they think about others. One day, I was folding flyers for our candidate and overheard him saying, "Do you see how these idiots work?" I told myself you need these idiots to win an election. Now you see how you can do without me. I left the party and looked for another venue. The only other party that I thought would listen to my problems was the FN (Interview 27).

Although it is more common for individuals with a right-wing or conservative ideology to slowly drift towards more radical ideas, two cases in my sample involved people adhering to a leftist ideology who became attuned to the ideas of the FN. For Daniel, this switching of political camps was linked to a concrete occurrence, which he explains as follows:

> My father was a socialist, who was friends with the socialist Prime Minister Pierre Bérégovoy. Thanks to him, I have always been attached to the social aspect of politics. However, when, during my studies, I saw the destroyed walls and the vandalism at the philosophy faculty in Lyon, which was conducted by left-wing anarchists in the 1970s, I could not identify with leftist currents any more. I started to do some reading and became close to the nationalist rightist current, *La nouvelle droite*. (Interview 26)

5.2.2.5 Other Socialization Mechanisms

The four socialization mechanisms outlined above do not form a definitive list. To the contrary, there are more ways in which individuals come to adopt and support the goals and values of the FN. The party's leader, Marine Le Pen, as a charismatic and convincing figure, seems to have played a major role for some members. For example, for three new members, the FN and Marine Le Pen present the alternative, a different force that puts the people first and is not based on clientelism and corrupt networks. Jean-Luc epitomizes this type of member, who used to be disillusioned and apolitical but has found political hope thanks to Marine Le Pen.

For a long time, I had a very bad image of politics, I saw parties as clientelistic networks in which people give and receive favours. I also did not take Jean-Marie Le Pen seriously. However, Marine impresses me; in addition to being a good speaker, she uses lots of factual evidence to back up her points.

Jean-Luc's example shows that the FN's positioning as the alternative to what the members derogatorily label "UMPS" (the conglomerate between the PS and the UMP) might be successful in convincing (potential) members that activism in the ranks of the party can be a worthwhile endeavour. Although it is simplistic, the FN programme portrays the vision of a strong, united, and glorious France, with a charismatic leader and a programme that puts the people at the centre of all actions. Not only is this vision embraced by traditional members, it can also attract newcomers.

5.3 The Activists' Political Values

Characterizing right-wing activists based on their degree of radicalization, the literature distinguishes between extremists and moderates (see Klandermans and Mayer 2006; Mudde 2010; Art 2011). Art (2011: 32) describes the extremist category as activists devoted to ideology; they use violence as a means to either spontaneously or intentionally intimidate their "enemies" (such as Muslim immigrants or supporters of economic liberalism). They are revolutionary and against parliamentary democracy; they believe strongly in the establishment of a new authoritarian order and share neo-Nazi and Fascist discourses. "Moderates" are less radical activists. These individuals generally support the democratic order but would give less power to institutions. They defend their nation and culture against the invasion of immigrants, adhere to an ethno-pluralistic world view, and glorify the native country's history, culture, and traditions. Their discourses are anti-pluralist and sometimes have an overtly or covertly racist touch (Klandermans and Mayer 2006; Art 2011).

The literature on the radical right in France describes FN members as moderates with possibly some radical or extremist elements. Crépon (2012: 46) argues that they have moved away from the "biological racism" (47) that they preached in 1972. He posits that they believe in the superiority of one nationality over another, but this belief is not supported by any type of racial superiority. Rather, they claim that individuals with a different origin, religion, and culture cannot peacefully live together. In Crépon's (2012: 56) view, the most important danger in the minds of FN activists continues to be the immigrant or "stranger", who is responsible for the social and political problems that France is currently experiencing (a decline in international standing, a loss of national identity and sovereignty, and, most importantly, an invasion of foreigners and Muslim immigrants). Members of the FN define being *français*—French—as traditional and based largely on family heritage. Immigrants or strangers bring a foreign religion, culture, and way of living to France; as such they cannot be considered truly French and pose a threat to the survival of the French nation state. To underline this point, Crépon (2006) quotes

Bruno Mégret, who argued in 1990 that "in the history of mankind there is no example of peaceful and durable coexistence between different ethnic and religious communities".

To complement Crépon (2006, 2012), Bizeul (2003) describes that the foundational belief of many FN members is the notion of the "perfect society" (18). FN members aim to restore society to its natural order. According to Bizeul, the FN offers an image of an open community for people of all ethnicities, but in reality all members are strongly against immigration and aim for a "model society" that consists only of *le peuple français* (19). Bizeul (2003: 35) adds that the FN justifies its actions and beliefs on the basis that the political organization in power was unjustly elected and that intervention is required to save France from political ruin (35).

My interview research confirms these descriptions of the FN membership. In the eyes of the FN members, (Muslim) immigration is the top threat that France is currently facing. Immigrants undermine France's cultural and political heritage, destroy the social system, impose their foreign Muslim religion on France and its people, and create insecurity in the public realm. Lucie expresses this feeling quite radically:

> We have an overpopulation of immigrants. There are too many foreigners that come and impose their culture and their way of living in France. Coloured people, who come from who knows where, assault us every minute. You cannot walk through the street quietly any more. Because France is paying so much for all these immigrants, single mums do not have the means to get enough money to make ends meet. These immigrants bring us nothing. We are invaded by them. They also have a lot of babies. This aggravates the problem, because we also have to pay for them. (Interview 42)

The way that FN members describe immigrants from Northern Africa follows Huntington (1996). Without referencing him or knowing who he is, three interviewees used the term "clash of civilizations" to describe their relationship with foreigners. According to Paul,

> There are two populations that live in France right now, which do not have the same ideology, values, and religion. One population is an Islamic population that arrives from Muslim countries; the other population is our population, the French population. This clash of civilizations can only lead to civil war. Who can win, the population that outnumbers the other one; in other words, the real problem is a demographic problem. Currently, we are suffering from an invasion not by armies but by people.

As Paul indicated, when my interviewees discussed immigration, they almost exclusively referred to Muslim or North African immigration. They distinguished the more recent immigration waves from the early waves from Poland and Southern Europe. According to several FN members, these early immigrants, who came between the 1920s and 1950s, integrated and assimilated into the French society and now are quite indistinguishable from French natives. However, later waves of immigrants, mainly from North Africa, no longer tend to assimilate. Instead, they want to impose their lifestyle, culture, and traditions on the French population. Coupled with broad trends such as globalization and European integration, which further buttress immigration, these strangers are responsible for the loss of French identity and culture. Faced with the danger imposed by massive immigration and a hostile national and international environment, many of the interviewees naturally want to protect their lifestyle, culture, and identity, which have been historically formed by a set of customs, values, and beliefs.

To shelter "their" France and fight against this invasion by foreigners, FN members support what they call protective measures. The most popular of these is national priority or national preference in the attribution of jobs, housing, and social benefits. As noted in Chap. 3, the national preference advocates that jobs, housing, and social benefits should be given predominantly to French citizens. In other words, if two individuals apply for the same job, one without French nationality and one with French nationality, the job should be given to the latter regardless of whether he or she is more or less qualified for the job. As a second measure, many interviewees advocated modifications in the acquisition of the French nationality. In particular, the right of soil—that is, everybody who is born in France is automatically awarded French nationality—should be changed to the right of blood—that is, only children who have one parent with French nationality can become French.

As part of their overall strategy, FN activists advocate France's retreat from the European Union and Schengen, the propagation of protectionist policies, and the reindustrialization of France. They feel that they are no longer in charge of their own affairs, but are dependent on the neo-liberal, immigration-friendly policy propagated by the European Union and international financial institutions. According to Mathias, the European Union practises an open border policy, allows disloyal competition from the USA and China, and does not respect French interests (Interview 44). In the view of several FN members, France's elites, whether they adhere to a leftist or rightist ideology, and whether they are in the political, economic, or social sector, all support this Europeanized, globalized ideology. In Mathias's view, "These elites willingly perpetuate the decadence of France's culture, economy, and society. They are brainwashed by the dominant ideology, they do not think about the French people, but about their own wallet". Paul expresses this feeling even more drastically:

> In all they do Sarkozy and Hollande are co-pilots. Either of the two continues the same globalization and Europeanization policies. Neither of them turns right or left from this preconceived policy. The "UMPS" will drive France right against a wall. It is time that the FN takes the steering wheel, otherwise the country will crash. The FN is the only force that can change the directions of events. (Interview 18)

The FN members further perceive that the over-powerful political and social elites have corrupted the whole state. For example, many members complain about media bias. In their view, the journalists in France are not free but are guided by the establishment. They follow the propaganda of the dominant ideology and deliberately spread false information about social and political issues such as immigration, unemployment, and the real costs of European integration. Some members also have a disdain for the French education system, which brainwashes children. Showing me her 11-year-old daughter's textbook, Caroline argues,

Our national education system is a shame. Look at this textbook which has been done in conjunction with SOS racism. There are chapters entitled "fight racism" or "embrace foreign cultures." All these affirmations there are shocking. The sheer headline "fight racism" implies that there is racism in France. In addition, our children are encouraged to accept a multicultural world, a world where we should embrace foreign lifestyles, foreign food, and diverse religions, but nobody talks about the French culture, the fact that our lifestyle that has grown over hundreds of years is declining. Even worse, national education distorts history. Students can get their high school diploma without knowing who Louis XIV or Napoleon was. However, they learn about French Africa, but only from a negative lens. The connotation with which the word French Africa is used now is so bad that if you use the word it is nearly an insult. If this education continues to mislead our children as it does currently, our children will soon learn that we are responsible for the extinction of the dinosaurs. (Interview 16)

The FN members also believe in the marginalization and victimization discourse that is pushed by the FN establishment. They despise the political discourse that considers them racist. On average, the members maintain that despite all recent electoral successes, there are still prejudices within French society. In Stephanie's words, "Our program is not racist, our speeches are not racist and our actions are not racist either. However, people think that we are racist" (Interview 2). The FN members think that they embrace positions that are moderate. For example, they embrace the slogan "Neither right nor left" and call themselves the alternative that makes sense and that reforms the corrupt French political system from the bottom to the top.

FN members therefore yearn for a charismatic leader who stands above politics, frees them from all bonds and mediocrities, who will re-establish the country's former glory, solves unemployment, and, to use Marine le Pen's 2012 presidential campaign slogan, puts the people first. The members think that Marine Le Pen incorporates these qualities. She is independent, strong, and visionary and impresses with facts and nothing else. To express their admiration for her, some members, such as Marianne, say that they are honoured to fight on her side (Interview 34). For others, such as Claude, she incorporates "inspiration, political knowledge, and leadership" (Interview 10). One member, Stéphan, even sees prophetic qualities in Marine Le Pen. For him she simply incorporates the truth, a truth that he wants to follow (Interview 37). For Roger, the politicians of the mainstream elitist parties—Hollande, Ayrault, Chirac, Sarkozy—are dwarves (Interview 1), when compared with Marine Le Pen.[49]

In sum, the current members of the FN do not use a revisionist or neo-Nazi discourse. Rather they are moderates extremists, who aim to achieve their goals through peaceful means. However, classifying them as moderates does not mean that their views are moderate in the usual sense. Rather, some of their discourses are anti-pluralist, racist, and aggressive. Their ideal vision of France also differs dramatically from the country's current state of affairs. FN members want to transform the Fifth Republic into a populist democracy governed by Marine Le Pen.

---

[49] Almost all of my interviewees seem to have developed an emotional connection with Marine Le Pen, as evidenced by the fact that they call her by her first name.

In this populist democracy, Marine Le Pen would be *le roy du peuple* who gives France back its independence and glory. In her government, referenda would be a means to consult people, Muslim immigration would be curtailed, and France would leave the European Union and once again become a strong independent nation in which French nationals would be given preference in all economic, political, and social matters. This description of the FN members also clearly indicates that the membership under Marine Le Pen has not become more mainstream in terms of ideology than it was during her father's reign. Rather, the same goals, slogans, and values are still upheld by the party and its members, even though membership has quadrupled over the past 4 years.

5.4 The Activists' Personal Values

The literature on radical right-wing activists has so far largely neglected to discuss activists' personal motivations for engagement. Orfali (1991), LaFont (2001), and Bizeul (2003) hint that FN members' engagement in their party is driven by the strong wish to integrate French civil society and to contribute to a brighter future. For example, Bizeul (2003) explains that despite the various backgrounds of the FN members, newcomers join because they are eager to play a social role within the country (37). During my fieldwork, I found confirmation for Bizeul's observation. Beyond an urge to do something about France's economic, social, and political degradation, the FN activists in my sample also show some altruistic values, such as "I do this engagement to provide my children with a better life" are not uncommon among my interviewees (Interview 16). Moreover, the members perceive their engagement and dedication as a contribution to society. René says, simply, "Politics signifies to me that I take care of the people around me and that I honour my motherland" (Interview 13). For others, such as Sophie, joining the FN is an act of conscience (Interview 24).

Honesty and truth are very important personal qualities, which the current FN members closely associate with their engagement. My interviewees consider that by being engaged in the FN, they are also truthful to themselves. Claude expresses this conviction in the following way: There is a truth in politics and we represent it. We tell the French people what is wrong with our country (Interview 43). In this sense, the FN activists are proud that their leaders "correctly" predicted that Europeanization, immigration, and Islamization have posed insurmountable problems to the French state. For example, many members mention that the FN was the first party to discuss immigration and integration, and now these topics are on the agenda for all parties.

However, the activists' convictions and their pride in fighting on the right side of history are sometimes transformed into disdain for individuals and parties that do not think and act like they do. My interviewees also do not have a lot of appreciation for "citizens" who think as they do but do not have the courage to join the FN. Richard summarizes this thought as follows:

My environment amuses me. Some of the people I know respect me because I am in the Front and they think that I am courageous. However, these people are small, they have no convictions, and they do not want to do anything. I do not have a lot of respect for them, because they do not have the courage to join us (Interview 22).

5.5 The Activists' Motivations for Engagement

The literature on engagement in social movement organizations (e.g. Klandermans 1986, 1997, 2004) cites three motivations for activists to become and stay engaged in radical right-wing groups: instrumentality, identity, and ideology. Instrumentality refers to individuals who elect to participate in a radical right-wing group because they believe that they can change the social and political environment. Besides some ideological convergence between his or her personal convictions, a (potential) activist must also see or believe that his or her own actions can change empirical realities (Lichbach 1994). Identity, or the awareness of belonging to a valued group, is the second motivating factor for radical right-wing activists. According to Klandermans and Mayer (2006), identity defines an "in-group" that members identify with and an "out-group" from which they distance themselves (9). Activists gain a positive social identity from their participation in the social movement and thus feel committed to the movement, its other members, and its leader (9). Ideology constitutes the third motivating factor for right-wing extremist participation and refers to members engaging in political discourse and expressing their views (Stekelenburg and Klandermans 2007). The ideology motif is often linked to emotions. Individuals for participation in a radical right-wing group—or any other social movement, for that matter—because they express to show their indignation at a particular state of affairs (Goodwin 2001; Goodwin et al. 2004). The more strongly people feel about an issue or ideology, the more likely that it is that they show continued (strong) involvement.

The more general literature on members in radical right-wing organizations, as well as the more specific literature on the FN, concurs that the ideology and identity motifs are very important to activists' involvement in a group like the FN. For example, Klandermans and Mayer (2006: 9) see ideology as a key motivational factor in explaining individuals' sustained involvement. In their view, right-wing groups are "carriers of meaning, which through processes such as 'consensus mobilization' or 'framing' seek to propagate their definition of the situation to the public at large" (9). They further argue that the radical right-wing movement provides a fruitful environment for activists to exchange experiences and tell their stories and a forum through which individuals can act on their beliefs (10). Others, such as Goodwin et al. (2012), point out that group identity processes are essential for members' sustained involvement. According to these authors, members of radical right-wing groups form a cohesive and loyal unit that provides funding, labour, access to wider networks of supporters, and linkages to grassroots opinions. Still other authors, such as Klandermans (2013) and Von Mering and McCarty (2013), add that stigmatization by family members, close friends,

5.5 The Activists' Motivations for Engagement

state institutions, or other social movements fosters in-group cohesion. Individuals within the movement often befriend each other and also spend non-political free time together.

The literature on the FN confirms this picture. From Bizeul's (2003) perspective, the FN is a "community of victims" (19)—outcasts who find refuge within the party and consequently possess a strong sense of solidarity with each other. He further argues that French people join the FN because they wish to belong to a social group and find the FN accessible and easy to join in an increasingly closed society (37). Concurring with Bizeul (2003), Crépon (2012) adds that FN members justify their actions and beliefs on the basis of their moral indignation against the political organization in power that is unjustly elected, the French elites that drive the country into political ruin, and immigrants who aim not only to milk France's social system but to also orientalize French society.

My interview data mainly confirm this picture. Ideology or the belief that they are on the right side of history is a driving factor behind almost all members' engagement. No member who I talked to could imagine leaving the party for political expediency. For example, Marianne explains her conviction as follows: "If we win or not, I always want to continue. We are not in the FN to have a mandate but to spread our ideas" (Interview 34). Paul adds that "those who give up are those who have come for personal reasons; real activists keep on fighting whatever happens" (Interview 20). Some members also stress that in contrast to members of other parties, they are "real activists", Stéphan nicely summarizes this point: "It is not an easy way to be engaged in the FN, you are not engaged in the Socialist Party and you are not engaged to advance your political career" (Interview 37). It is also telling that regardless of whether they are strongly or weakly involved, none of my interview partners could imagine leaving the party, expect if they were to feel betrayed by the party elite. However, they cannot imagine that this would happen. Rather, they are proud to represent the FN and Marine Le Pen and see it as their duty to fight for their convictions. For example, Arno affirms that if he were to give up his activism he would no longer be able to look at himself in the mirror in the mornings (Interview 27). Similar, it is natural for Clemens, who considers himself a Catholic nationalist, to fight with and for the FN. Even more pronounced, Catharine affirms that "only death can stop me from being engaged" (Interview 14).

Coupled with the ideology motif, a strong sense of group identity is primordial for FN activists. FN members feel at ease within their party. They enjoy the open climate within the organization, the interaction with other members, and the many events that the FN offers for its members.[50] It seems that for some members, joining the FN was a process of cognitive liberation (see McAdam 1982). Joining a group of like-minded people, they no longer feel marginalized but may come to feel recognized, popular, and valued. The FN also offers them an environment to express their views, which turns the organization into a very appealing place to

---

[50]This feature is quite astonishing given that the FN has a very hierarchical structure modelled after communist parties.

spend their free time. In fact, it was not uncommon for my interviewees to refer to the FN as "a second family", a kind of counter-society in which people interact with one another beyond politics; they make friends and acquaintances and sometimes even find their partner for life there.

Part of the reason that the FN still forms such a cohesive in-group might lie in the continued discrimination against FN members in their daily social and professional lives. Despite Marine Le Pen's continued efforts of *de-diabolization* and despite the fact that approximately half of the French population now considers the FN "a party like others", more than 50 % of the FN activists I talked to still claim to have faced some professional or personal disadvantages as a direct result of their involvement with the FN. Such stigmatization is certainly less pronounced than it was 10 or 20 years ago, but it is still there. For example, to avoid being branded as an FN member at work, 10 of my interviewees have not made their FN membership public. However, this does not mean that they are not active; rather, some members work undercover or in the shadows to support their ideology, goals, and party. Jérôme is probably the most active of these hidden FN members, who have not yet "come out". Anonymously and with a fake profile, he runs one of the largest FN Facebook pages in France. When asked why he keeps his involvement secret, he states, "publicly declaring your affiliation with the FN means an immediate stop to your professional career" (Interview 19).

Pertaining to their personal life, more than half of the activists who have made their membership in the FN public stated that they have lost friends and acquaintances, have had trash thrown in their backyard, or their children were insulted by their peers. Several members also complained about verbal and physical violence. For example, Marianne told me that on several occasions, when she dropped off her children in school, she was insulted by some of her son's classmates: "Fascist, how many Arabs did you kill today" (Interview 34), and two members claim to have been physically attacked while putting up posters in problematic districts.

Although the discrimination that many members face in their daily lives makes some individuals think twice before deciding to join the FN, it helps to foster the cohesion of the movement. People like to bond with people who think, act, and feel similarly. The continuing stigmatization also allows FN members to present themselves as victims of a corrupt system that discriminates against them despite the fact that they, the FN activists, accept the rules of the game. This stigmatization also strengthens their beliefs. They embrace the FN's anti-system attitude and are proud that they are the alternative, an alternative that is neither right nor left but incorporates the good sense of the people. Hence, the stigmatization that FN members still perceive, either latently or physically, not only helps them create a coherent in-group but helps to strengthen the activists' ideological beliefs.

5.6 Engagement Trajectory

Despite the fact that the activists praise the grass-roots character of the FN, the party was and remains a hierarchical organization. Except for periodic elections of the party leader, intra-party elections have been nonexistent. For over 40 years, members who want to advance their careers within the movement need to be promoted. To gain responsibility at the local level, they must be promoted by the departmental secretary. To obtain any office beyond the local level, they must be appointed by the national leadership or the leader—Jean-Marie Le Pen until 2011 and Marine Le Pen thereafter. (It has also been up to the party leader to exclude members; the FN's executive bureau, which is occupied by those faithful to the leader, has normally rubberstamped any decision taken by Jean-Marie Le Pen or Marine Le Pen.)

However, despite this hierarchical conception, the FN has been a party composed of activists. Except for some members of the national leadership (such as Florian Philippot), all individuals started at the local level. Under the leadership of both Jean-Marie Le Pen and Marine Le Pen, the members integrate into a departmental and, if existent, local chapter and start off as true "activists", distributing flyers, putting up posters, and participating in local meetings.[51] Under Jean-Marie Le Pen, when the party had a lack of human resources—which was most pronounced after the split in the late 1990s—it was possible for members to advance very quickly and gain responsibilities weeks or months after joining the movement. Even though many members still do not want to make their FN membership public, the activist pool has increased under Marine Le Pen, who, since taking office in 2011, has also tried to promote individuals with relevant skills and knowledge. Those who are committed, have proven activist credentials, and are able to defend the ideas of the movement can advance relatively quickly up the party ranks. In fact, it has not been uncommon in public for new members to become candidates for electoral office only months after joining the party, although lingering stigmatization makes many members hesitant about or resistant to running for elected office. Therefore, the party is constantly searching for competent candidates to represent the party on local or regional lists.

---

[51] However following Marine Le Pen's victory in 2011, existing local chapters have attracted more members and new chapters have spread. On the departmental level, the FN has also professionalized. Many departmental branches now have a headquarters with meeting rooms, office spaces, and infrastructure such as computers, faxes, and telephones. However, these headquarters are still run by activists. None of the departmental offices has any paid staff.

5.7 Changes in Membership Under Marine Le Pen: A Synopsis

The FN under Marine Le Pen has made impressive gains in terms of human resources. Compared to her predecessor and father Jean-Marie Le Pen, Marine Le Pen has not only managed to more than triple the party's membership between 2011 and 2014, she has also broadened its appeal. The FN no longer attracts predominantly the so-called losers of modernization—low-income individuals who cannot cope with the rapidly changing Europeanized and globalized world order. It is now a more of a catch party that attracts individuals from different social classes, various education levels, and a variety of professions. Members are young and old, men and women, divorced and married, and citizens who have come to embrace the values and goals of the FN through various mechanisms (such as family socialization by activist parents, socialization in school or university, socialization through formative events in adult life or through general dissatisfaction with the mainstream right).

It is impressive that the FN has become "catch-all" without changing its values. Rather than making the FN less radical and more mainstream, the current FN members, whether recent or longstanding, strongly engaged or weakly engaged, male or female, embrace the same values that the FN has traditionally embraced. They incorporate the typical ideology of radical right-wing parties: they see it as their mission to protect their motherland France, sheltering it as one would protect a human body from viruses. These "viruses" are immigrants, who are perceived as an economic, criminal, and demographic threat; Islam, which is perceived as an aggressive and expansionist religion that wants to eradicate Catholicism, more particularly, and Christianity more generally; the European Union, which strips France of its sovereignty and propagates detrimental polices in the social and economic realm; and economic liberalism and globalization, which are responsible for outsourcing and the race to the bottom of the French economy. Instead of these vices, FN members propose protectionist and nationalist policies, more authoritarian values, and a popular democracy run by Marine Le Pen.

The FN members are very united in these fights. Paul describes this unity as follows:

> Inside the FN we are bunch of different people similar to the Gallic people in the cartoon "Asterix" and "Obelix". Yet, we have some common convictions and we are ready to fight for these convictions. These common convictions are summarized around the necessity to protect the nation state. We might disagree about many things inside the FN, but once our France is attacked we will defend it with the same force as the Gallic tribes defended their country against the Roman invasions (Interview 20).

In addition to displaying the same values, FN activists appreciate themselves within the organization. They take pleasure in the fact that they can express their opinions openly and without discrimination. They see the FN as a second family. The close ties with other members compensate for the stigmatization in real life. The pleasure that activists experience within the FN, coupled with their

5.7 Changes in Membership Under Marine Le Pen: A Synopsis

ideologically driven commitment, is also strongly motivating for many members. This motivation translates into the many hours (in some cases up to 6 or 7 hours a day) that the activists spend in and for the party, without receiving any compensation.

In short, the FN has become a "Volksparty", by attracting more than 80,000 members. The movement has consolidated its third-place position among French political parties. The members carry the FN traditional message and show a high degree of ideological commitment and attachment to the party. Thanks to them, the FN is now more strongly implemented at the local level, even if many of the members still do not want to run on FN lists. In short, as of 2015, the party has the critical mass of activists to run the daily business of the party, convince others to join or vote for the party, and propagate the FN's message.

Chapter 6
The FN Voters Under Jean-Marie Le Pen and Marine Le Pen

Electorally, the FN reached new heights after Marine Le Pen took over the FN presidency in 2011. Most notably, in the 2012 presidential election, she nearly doubled the vote achieved by her father, Jean-Marie Le Pen, 5 years before, by winning 18 % of the vote. The subsequent municipal and European elections allowed the FN to further consolidate this electoral result (Goodliffe 2012: 137). In the 2014 municipal elections, the FN won the majority of votes in 12 towns and elected 1534 councillors. In the European Parliament elections in May 2014, the FN achieved the best result in the party's history, winning an unprecedented 25 % of the vote, making it the most successful party in that election (Laubacher 2014). Finally, in the March 2015 departmental elections, the FN confirmed the result obtained in the European Parliament elections; again the party won 25 % of the vote (see Fig. 6.1).

In this chapter, I ask where these new votes have come from. Has the FN attracted new voters, or has the party been more successful tapping into its traditional voter base? The literature on the electoral success of the FN is split with regard to these questions. Perrineau (2012: 2) argues that in the 40-year history of the party, the FN electorate has not changed. He claims that the FN vote has been strong among men, young people, the working class, and individuals with little education, the so-called losers of modernization. Others such as Mayer (1998) and Hainsworth (2004) contest this claim. According to Mayer (1998: 8), the FN under Jean-Marie Le Pen drew on diverse categories of the voting public, and these categories fluctuated over time.

I hypothesize that if the FN electorate fluctuates or broadens, it should particularly change at a time of internal and external reshuffles. Internally, with the election of Marine Le Pen, the FN has become younger and more dynamic. As noted in Chap. 3, the party has also changed its message, albeit more in form than in content. It packages its populist anti-immigrant positions within a republican discourse. Externally, there is a specific economic, social, and political climate that should benefit the party electorally. Economically, France has not recovered from the crisis that started to cripple the country in 2009. Socially, parts of France's

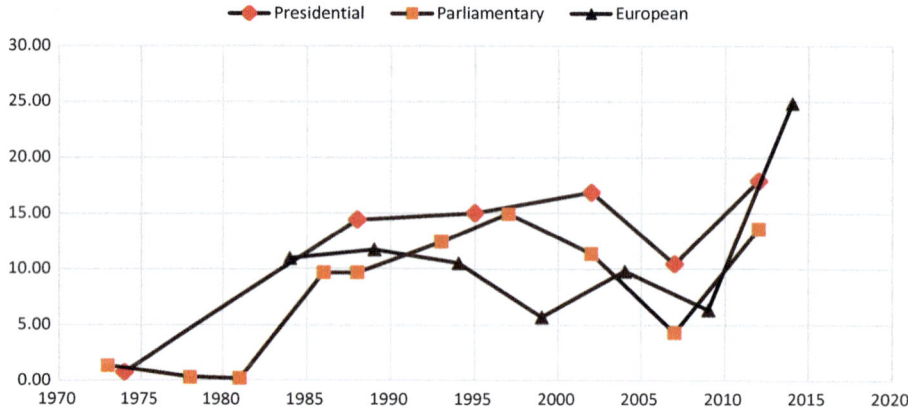

Fig. 6.1 Evolution of the FN vote, 1973–2014. Source: Lecoeur and Poulterniez 2013; Site du *Ministère de l'intérieur* 2015a, b

population suffer from an identity crisis, and they perceive the FN's claim of a threat emanating from the Muslim religion and North African immigration as real. Politically, France is also in a crisis. Throughout 2013, 2014, and 2015, President Hollande's popularity had been at a record low in the polls, and the moderate right, the UMP, not faring much better. Therefore, I assume that if there is a change or broadening in the FN electorate, it is likely that this change will happen at a time of internal and structural changes.

Below, I attempt to determine the degree to which the FN electorate has changed under Marine Le Pen. To do so, I try to determine the typical FN voter's profile in 2007 and in 2012 using data from the *Comparative Study of Electoral Systems* (CSES). Specifically, I aim to evaluate whether the influence on the FN vote of socio-professional status, education, gender, age, area of residence, religious practice, and assessment of democracy (Tiberj 2012) differs in 2012 from 2007. I first present the constituents of the FN vote and formulate hypotheses for how various predictors behaved differently in 2012 than in 2007. Second, I present the methods and data used for this chapter. Third, I explain and situate the results.

6.1 Predictors of the FN Electoral Success

The literature (Arzheimer and Carter 2009; Arzheimer 2012) concurs that the electoral success of radical right-wing parties such as the FN is triggered by demographics, socio-economic factors, and attitudinal factors. To present the predictor variables of the FN vote, I follow these three categories.

6.1.1 Demographics

I include three demographics: gender, age, and marital status. With regard to the first variable, gender, radical right-wing parties have traditionally attracted a male electorate. For example, like other radical right-wing parties, in the 1980s and 1990s, the FN propagated a conservative ideology based on family, the nation, and the protection of customs and traditions (Birenbaum 1992). As Kitschelt (2007: 1201) notes, these features, combined with the radical right's rejection of the progressive agenda of leftist parties, made women hesitant about or hostile to the FN's discourse. However, starting in the early 2000s, male support for the radical right in general, and the FN in particular, may be slightly less dominant. For example, Givens (2004: 48) reports that the gender gap in the radical right-wing vote narrowed in the early 2000s. More recent work (Mayer 2012, 2013, 2015) even suggests that there is no longer a gender gap in the FN vote. The FN under Marine Le Pen is more feminine, dynamic, and left-wing in social issues—all factors that might make the party as popular among women as among men now. Following Mayer (2012), I hypothesize that the FN was still more popular among men in 2007, but that by 2012 the gender gap in FN support had closed.

The second demographic factor is age. Traditionally, the FN, as the prototypical representative of the radical right, was particularly successful in attracting older individuals. The party's traditional and conservative ideology was said to be appealing to older individuals, who might have felt alienated in the fast-moving twentieth and early twenty-first centuries (Kessler and Freeman 2005: 265). Falter and Schumann's (1988: 104) simple statement "The older the people are, the more right-wing they seem to be" appeared to hold true for a long time for the FN vote. More recently, however, parties such as the FN have likely gained in popularity among the younger cohorts of the population. For example, both Hainsworth (2008) and Arzheimer (2012) report an overrepresentation of individuals aged 18–30 in the electorate of the radical right throughout Europe, including France. There may be many reasons for younger individuals to become increasingly attracted to the populist and nationalist discourse of the FN. Among others, these individuals no longer develop traditional ties to the established parties, suffer more and more from an insecure position in the labour market, and bear the brunt of the current economic crises. Based on these observations, I assume that the FN vote should be particularly high among young voters in 2012.

The third demographic variable is marital status. I assume an overrepresentation of married individuals within the FN electorate in 2007 and 2012, albeit more so in 2007. Werts et al. (2012: 186) provide a convincing theoretical reason that married individuals should be overrepresented in the FN electoral base. The FN strongly values and glorifies traditional institutions such as marriage and the family in its programme. However, I also suggest that this link should be less strong in 2012. Although marriage is still a sacred institution in the FN programme, in practice things have changed slightly. Not only is the FN leader Marine Le Pen divorced and currently living out of wedlock with FN vice president Louis Aliot, but there are also some homosexuals in the upper circles of the FN (e.g. Florian Philippot). Marine Le Pen also did not participate in the demonstrations against *le mariage pour tous* that occurred in 2013 and 2014. Because the party's traditional appeal was stronger in 2007, and because marriage as an institution was more strongly valued under Jean-Marie Le Pen, I assume that, if at all, marital status should have a stronger influence in 2007.

6.1.2 Socio-economic Factors

I add four socio-economic factors into the analysis: education, place of residency, professional status as worker, and employment status. As long as research on the constituents of the radical right-wing vote in Europe, and the FN vote more specifically, has existed, education has been one of the key variables in explaining why some individuals are more likely than others to support a populist right-wing party (see Stockemer 2012). The literature concurs that less-educated individuals might be more prone to be attracted to the discourse of the FN, which identifies a culprit (immigration and elites) and provides clear and simple solutions (the expulsion of immigrants and the reestablishment of national sovereignty). Individuals with less education as a group also suffer more from the effects of globalization, outsourcing, and the loss of low-skilled jobs than do individuals who are well off. These so-called losers of modernization are the least apt to keep up with the demands of modern society (see Mayer 2013: 162). Hence, of all citizens, individuals with low educational attainment might value the shifts to globalized high-tech societies and pluralistic lifestyles the least. In contrast, highly educated citizens, who as a group have disproportionately profited from globalization, tend to also embrace cultural diversity, post-materialism, and individualistic lifestyles (Kitschelt 2007: 1201). Empirical research overwhelmingly supports the notion that education is key in explaining variation in radical right-wing support. In Arzheimer's (2012: 44) words, "All national and comparative studies demonstrate that citizens with university education are least likely to vote for the extreme right". Mayer (2007: 434) confirms that intellectuals and students are the least likely to cast their ballot for the FN. Because the content of the FN programme did not change from 2007 to 2012, I assume that there should be a negative relationship between education and FN electoral support within the timeframe of this analysis; that is, the higher an individual's education level, the lower the likelihood that he or she will support the FN.

The second socio-economic factor that might influence an individual's likelihood to vote FN, albeit indirectly, is place of residency. I assume that the FN vote should be higher in the countryside than in cities or densely populated areas. As a rule, traditional values and a traditional lifestyle, religiosity, and attachment to the nation should be more strongly pronounced in rural areas than in cities (Ignazi 2003; Barone and Négrier 2015). In contrast, leftist or progressive parties should have an electoral edge in cities, as densely populated areas are generally characterized by a cosmopolitan, multicultural, and diverse environment. In the literature, this difference is most explicitly referred to in Bornschier (2005). According to him, the radical right has gained a strong footing in the countryside, as it is the only party family that defends national traditions and opposes multiculturalism. In particularly, mapping the FN electorate in France, Bussi and Fouquet (2007) report that rural and suburban zones significantly outnumber cities in FN support. For the purpose of this analysis, I follow Bussi and Fouquet (2007) and hypothesize that the FN finds a more propitious terrain among individuals who live in the countryside, which might entice them to cast their ballot for this radical right-wing party. I have no reason to believe that this relationship should be different from 2007 to 2012.

Third, I hypothesize that, in particular after Marine Le Pen took over the FN presidency, among all professional groups, workers should be the most likely to cast a vote for the FN. Favouring a neo-liberal economic agenda, the FN started off as a party of the petit bourgeoisie in the 1970s and 1980s. It tried to attract a traditional conservative electorate, such as farmers and the self-employed (Hameau 1992: 101). Yet, starting in the 1990s and 2000s, the FN abandoned its neo-liberal platform and incorporated leftist elements. With Marine Le Pen taking over the party's presidency, this shift towards socialist ideas, albeit with a nationalistic twist, has become central to the FN's programme (Ivaldi 2015). For example, in Marine Le Pen's 2012 programme, she aggressively advocates wage increases for modest incomes, the reindustrialization of France, and the protection of French workers against disloyal foreign competition (Mayer 2012; Bussi et al. 2012).

Not only has the FN targeted its programme to the needs of workers, but the structural conditions in France should also make workers attuned to the FN rhetoric. Workers, as a group, suffer disproportionately from globalization processes, economic dislocations, and the fall of economic borders. Aside from a fragmented and divided left, the radical right in France (and elsewhere) is the only party family that condemns these economic developments (Oesch 2008: 315). Given that manual labour jobs are the type of jobs that face most foreign competition, the FN's strategy to scapegoat foreigners might sit particularly well with these workers (Kitschelt 2007: 1200). Givens (2004: 50) summarizes this point quite well: "Blue-collar workers [are] more likely to be anti-immigrant than those in other sectors".

Fourth, I follow the literature and assume that individuals in the most precarious economic situation (the unemployed) will be more likely to vote FN than will individuals in an economically comfortable situation (see, e.g. Clark and Legge 1997). I further conjecture that after several consecutive years of economic crises (with unemployment rates reaching 10 %), the frustration of the most vulnerable should be particularly strong. Hence, in 2012, the unemployed might be particularly receptive to the FN's discourse, which offers an alternative to the main parties' programmes—a platform based on populism, the reindustrialization of France, and the national preference in the allocation of jobs (Loch and Heitmeyer 2001). In addition, policies that favour multiculturalism, immigration, and open borders might not sit well with a constituency that suffers from economic degradation (Rouban 2013: 6). Based on these considerations, I assume that the unemployed were more likely to vote FN in 2012 than in 2007.

6.1.3 Attitudinal Factors

I add two attitudinal variables—religiosity and individuals' satisfaction with democracy—to the list of possible predictors of the FN vote in 2007 and 2012. First, I expect more-religious individuals to be more likely to vote FN than less-religious individuals (Tiberj 2012: 71). Although it is true that the xenophobic and inegalitarian message of the FN is rejected by France's Christian churches, it is also true that the FN has traditionally appealed to very religious or fundamentalist Catholics (Mayer 2013: 163). Immerzeel et al. (2013: 962) support the notion that fundamentalist Christians find an ideological home within the radical right. According to them, orthodox or very strong believers in the Christian ideology are generally very traditional and conservative. Hence, they should have a high likelihood to vote for a party such as the FN. In contrast, tolerant believers and non-believers should probably be less traditional and more post-materialist, making them less likely to support the FN. I also hypothesize that the level of religiosity should play a larger role under Jean-Marie Le Pen, who was more strongly anchored into a traditional Catholic milieu than is Marine Le Pen.

The second attitudinal factor is level of satisfaction with democracy. I hypothesize that the more individuals are dissatisfied with the state of democracy in France, the more likely they will vote for the FN. When it comes to the features that characterize France's democracy, the FN is an anti-system party. It rejects political and economic liberalism, the economic and political elites in France and internationally, and the European Union and European integration. The literature concurs that anti-system parties should profit from increased latent or real dissatisfaction with the system in place (Balent 2012). For example, in Oesch's (2008) view, individuals' assessment of how well democracy works in their country is the strongest predictor of the radical right-wing vote, overall. Similar, Kessler and Freeman (2005) advance that dissatisfaction with the regime, or with the actors that represent it, has a stronger value in predicting the radical right-wing vote than does socio-demographics.

I hypothesize that dissatisfaction with democracy should play a larger role in 2012 than in 2007. For one, Sarkozy, with his discourse on law and order and his promises to create jobs and undertake structural reforms, energized the conservative electorate in 2007. Yet, when he left office in 2012, he left parts of his (former) electorate disillusioned, because he did not deliver on what he promised. This may have left the conservative electorate resentful, not only of former president Sarkozy but of the system as a whole. In addition, the ongoing economic crisis, which the political actors in France have not curtailed, might also make more and more French individuals dissatisfied and in search of an alternative. This alternative could well be the FN.

6.2 Data

To determine which, if any, of the eight factors influenced FN voters in 2007 and 2012, I used data for France from the *Comparative Study of Electoral Systems* (CSES). To have a basis for comparison between 2007 and 2012, I have slightly changed some original coding to ensure that all variables are measured in the same way in the two datasets. The dependent variable—voted for the FN—is a dummy coded 1 for all survey respondents who indicated that they voted FN and 0 otherwise. I exclude individuals who did not vote from the analysis. The independent variables are coded as follows: first, gender is a dichotomous variable coded 0 for women and 1 for men. To code the second demographic factor, age, I distinguish four categories of adults: young (aged 18–34), middle-aged (aged 35–49), rather elderly (50–64), and elderly (65 and up). I created these categories because theory predicts that the relationship between age and the FN vote might well be not linear. Rather, it is likely that the FN vote is particularly high among the young, and possibly the elderly. The use of these four categories allows me to determine the degree to which this is the case. In the analysis that follows, I use three dummy variables for middle-aged, rather elderly, and elderly. The reference category is young adults.

I operationalize the third variable, marital status, by a dummy variable. I code all individuals who are married or living in a marriage-like relationship 1 and all other survey respondents 0. For the first socio-economic variable, education, I distinguish three categories: primary education, secondary education, and tertiary education. I capture these three categories in an ordinal variable. Individuals whose education level is a primary degree or lower (i.e. individuals who have completed *Le Collège* but have no higher degree) are coded 1, individuals who have completed High School of *le Lycée* are coded 2, and individuals who have any kind of university degree are coded 3). To account for place of residency, I use a four-item ordinal variable. Individuals who indicate that they live in the countryside are coded 1; in a small city, 2; in the suburbs of a large city, 3; and in a large city, 4. The two remaining socio-economic variables are dummy variables. First, I code workers 1 and individuals belonging to any other profession 0. Second, I code individuals who self-identify as unemployed 1 and all others 0.

The final two attitudinal variables are operationalized by ordinal variables. The first variable is a four-item indicator ranging from 1, "not religious at all", to 4, "very religious". The two intermediate categories are "not very religious" and "somewhat religious". The final variable, satisfaction with democracy, also has four categories: "very satisfied" (coded 1), "somewhat satisfied" (coded 2), "somewhat dissatisfied" (coded 3), and "very dissatisfied" (coded 4).

6.3 Method

I present the analysis in two steps. First, I present some descriptive statistics of the dependent and independent variables. Second, and more importantly, I display the results of two multiple regression models, one for 2007 and one for 2012. Because the dependent variable is binary, I use two binary logistic regressions. On the left-hand side of the equation is the dichotomous variable "voted for the FN"; on the right-hand side are the nine theoretically informed covariates. Because the maximum likelihood estimation does not allow me to directly interpret the substantive influence of the regression coefficients, I transform the regression coefficients, which are presented in log odds in the regression output, into probabilities. To do so, I use Clarify, a programme developed by Michael Tomz, Jason Wittenberg, and Gary King (Tomz et al. 2003).

6.4 Results

The descriptive statistics (see Table 6.1) reveal some interesting results. First, and most strikingly, there are vast differences in the underreporting of the FN vote. In 2007, only slightly over 3 % of the survey respondents indicated that they voted FN. Compared to the 10.45 % of the vote that Jean-Marie Le Pen received, this illustrates that two out of three respondents who actually voted FN did not acknowledge this in the survey. Yet, the same underreporting is no longer present in 2012. Rather, when asked which party they voted for, more than 15 % admitted/indicated that they voted FN in the 2012 presidential election. The underreporting

Table 6.1 Descriptive statistics[a]

	Mean 2007	Std. dev. 2007	Mean 2012	Std. dev. 2012
FN vote	0.032	0.175	0.151	0.360
Gender	0.424	0.494	0.477	0.500
Young adult	0.148	0.355	0.135	0.342
Middle-aged adult	0.316	0.466	0.305	0.461
Rather elderly adult	0.326	0.469	0.300	0.459
Elderly adult	0.211	0.408	0.260	0.439
Marital status	0.683	0.466	0.636	0.481
Education	2.24	0.678	2.19	0.668
Place of residency	2.79	1.27	2.06	1.03
Worker	0.142	0.349	0.529	0.500
Unemployed	0.046	0.210	0.072	0.258
Religiosity	2.12	0.925	2.02	0.923
Dissatisfaction with democracy	2.31	0.729	2.29	0.677

[a]I include observations only when there are no missing data for all variables. The number of observations (N) is 1579 for 2007 and 1466 for 2012

of the FN vote was merely around 3 % points. In other words, 80 % of the FN voters were sincere when indicating their vote choice in the survey. To piggyback on the findings from Chap. 3, this figure alone provides evidence that the *dédiabolisation* strategy undertaken by Marine Le Pen and the party has borne fruit. FN voters are now open about their vote choice and do not hide it any more.

Except for the underreporting in the FN vote, there is very little difference with regard to the descriptive statistics between 2007 and 2012. With the exception of the "worker" and "unemployed" categories—in 2012, as compared to 2007, many more individuals self-identified as being a worker and about double the number acknowledged that they were unemployed—the survey respondents are very much alike with regard to demographics, educational attainment, place of residency, and level of religiosity in 2007 and 2012, making the results of the multivariate regression models that ensue comparable. Even with regard to the final variable—individuals' satisfaction with democracy—there is basically no difference between 2007 and 2012. Yet, the question remains whether more religious individuals, individuals who live in the countryside, or those who are more dissatisfied with how democracy works in France were more likely to vote FN in 2012 than in 2007.

The results from the two regression analyses (see Table 6.2) indicate that there is relatively little difference in the profile of the FN voter between 2007 and 2012. Despite the fact that in 2012, 70 % more voters cast their ballot for the French radical right and despite the fact that in 2012 there was basically no underreporting in the CSES survey on the FN vote, I get a relatively similar picture in 2007 and 2012 with regard to the typical FN voter. In both election years, the FN support was significantly higher among individuals with little education, among workers,

Table 6.2 Results of the two logistic regression analyses for 2007 and 2012

	Model 2007	Model 2012
Gender	0.083 (0.310)	−0.206 (0.156)
Middle-aged	−0.471 (0.452)	−0.413* (0.232)
Rather elderly	−0.301 (0.458)	−0.464* (0.238)
Elderly	−0.549 (0.554)	−0.964 (0.284)
Marital status	0.799 (0.386)	0.080 (0.164)
Education	−0.509*** (0.250)	−0.469*** (0.156)
Place of residency	−0.119 (0.117)	−0.194** (0.080)
Worker	0.939*** (0.334)	0.665*** (0.191)
Unemployed	0.814 (0.521)	−0.579 (0.352)
Religiosity	0.036 (0.171)	−0.035 (0.085)
Dissatisfaction with democracy	0.641*** (0.191)	0.409*** (0.065)
Constant	−4.28 (1.13)	−1.04 (0.632)
Pseudo rsquared	0.10	0.10
Log likelihood	−200.34	−567.08

Standard errors in parentheses, $*p < 0.01$, $**p < 0.05$, $***p < 0.001$ (two tailed)

and among those who were dissatisfied with how democracy works in France. Yet, aside from these commonalities in the FN support structure, there are two differences between the two election years. First, the FN was more successful in attracting the young vote in 2012. Whereas the FN vote was relatively evenly split among all age cohorts in 2007, model 2 illustrates that Marine Le Pen's vote came more strongly from young individuals than from other age cohorts. Second, in 2012, the FN was electorally more successful in the countryside than in urban areas. This second finding is slightly surprising considering that the party under Marine Le Pen has become somewhat more modern and dynamic. Yet, rural areas suffered the most from the economic crisis. It may also be that fear of immigrants as competitors on the labour market and as a cultural threat is highest in rural areas (see also Lucassen and Lubbers 2012).

To highlight the edge that the FN gained among the young and individuals living in the countryside in 2012, I conducted some probability transformations of model 2. For the first of these two variables, age, the probability transformations illustrate that age plays a substantial role. Holding everything else at the median, model 2 forecasts that young adults aged 18–34 have a 22 % likelihood to vote FN; the two middle categories (individuals aged 35–49 and 50–64), an approximately 15 % likelihood to vote FN; and the elderly, a mere 10 % likelihood. In this sense, it is also worth noting that the elderly have the lowest probability to vote FN. This indicates that the traditional pattern of FN support has switched. For the second finding on the place of residency, model 2 predicts that a middle-aged man (aged 35–49), all of whose other attributes are at the median, has an 11 % likelihood to vote for the FN if he lives in a city and a higher than 18 % likelihood if he lives in the countryside. For young individuals (18–34), the model predicts an even larger gap (from a 15 % likelihood for somebody who lives in the city to a 25 % chance for somebody living in a rural area).

However, beyond strengthening its vote base with young voters and individuals living in the countryside, the FN electorate did not diversify in 2012. Rather, Marine Le Pen's party attracted votes from its core constituency; individuals with low education and citizens who are dissatisfied with democracy still figure most strongly among FN supporters. In fact, survey respondents who belong to either of these two cohorts were much more likely to vote FN in 2012 than in 2007, even if I take into account the strong underreporting of the FN vote in Jean-Marie Le Pen's last presidential bid. For example, model 1 predicts that, in 2007, a hypothetical young person with primary education (individual who left school at age 16) whose other characteristics were at the median had a slightly higher than 5 % likelihood to vote FN, or, if we account for the strong underreporting in the FN vote, a 16–17 % likelihood to vote for Jean-Marie Le Pen's party in 2007. In contrast, the odds for 2012 nearly doubled to 31 %.

For the indicator "dissatisfaction with democracy", the gap between the 2007 and 2012 presidential elections is perceptible, but somewhat less strong than for the "education" variable. Again holding everything else constant at the median, the likelihood for the hypothetical young adult to vote FN in 2007 increased from 2 % for individuals very satisfied with French democracy to slightly over 10 % for

6.4 Results

individuals who were very dissatisfied with French democracy. Taking the underreporting in the survey into consideration, these odds translate into a 5–6 % likelihood for satisfied citizens to vote Le Pen and a 30 % chance for dissatisfied citizens. For 2012, the probabilities for the same hypothetical person stand between 10 % for somebody very satisfied with democracy and 39 % for somebody very dissatisfied with democracy.

Finally, although the "worker" variable is significant in both models, the odds of somebody voting FN did not increase between 2007 and 2012. The predictions from model 1 indicate that a worker whose values for all other variables are at the median has a nearly 8 % chance to vote FN in 2007. If we consider the 2/3 underreporting, the odds increase to about 23 %, a number analogous to the probability transformation for the 2012 model. This finding at least tentatively indicates that the FN, although it continues to be overrepresented among workers, did not gain additional ground among this part of the population between 2007 and 2012.

It is also worth noting that I could not confirm the majority of the hypotheses that I initially postulated. Specifically, I find that that gender, religiosity, marital status, and economic hardship in the form of unemployment do not play a role in accounting for the FN vote either in 2007 or in 2012. For the first of these factors, gender, the two models predict that women were as likely to vote FN as men both in 2007 and in 2012. This allows for the tentative conclusion that the FN had closed the gender gap, at least when it comes to voting for this radical right-wing party, before Marine Le Pen took over the presidency. For religiosity the picture is similar. For both election years, religious individuals were neither more nor less likely to vote FN than were less-religious individuals. However, this does not necessarily mean that fundamentalist or orthodox Catholics, traditionally one of the core FN support groups, do not have a higher likelihood to vote FN. Rather, this group might be too small in numbers to have any influence in the survey.

The third factor, marital status, also does not significantly influence an individual's likelihood of voting FN. This result is probably the most expected, as marriage is supported not only by the FN but by all other parties and the state. Moreover, marriage is the most common form of cohabitation in France and Europe. The non-effect of unemployment is a little less expected. It does not provide support for the "crisis breeds extremism" hypothesis, at least for those who suffer the most from the crisis (the unemployed) (Rydgren and Ruth 2013). In fact, even in 2012, when the self-reported unemployment rate had nearly doubled from 2007, individuals in this most precarious economic situation were not more likely to vote FN than were individuals who work, study, or are retired. However, again this not mean that the FN has not profited from the crisis; it simply means that those who were most affected by the crisis had no higher or lower likelihood to vote FN than did the rest of the population.

6.5 Discussion

In contrast to FN membership, the party's vote base has not diversified as much. The largest part of the party's vote still comes from its traditional core: individuals with low educational attainment and citizens who are dissatisfied with how democracy works in France. On the one hand, despite the FN's elites' attempt to present themselves as a credible alternative to the two main parties, the UMP and the PS, this confirms the notion that the FN is still an anti-system party: against immigration, European integration, and what it calls corrupt domestic and international elites. On the other hand, this illustrates that the FN's programmatic refinement towards populism, a leftist political agenda, and the national preference sits very well with the popular electorate. This programmatic reorientation combined with the favourable structural environment, which is characterized by the ongoing economic crisis, the perception that the mainstream elites are corrupt, and some strong disconnect between the popular strata and the main parties, makes the FN attractive to those who feel alienated from the political system. While these popular strata do not necessarily include the unemployed, they do include workers and individuals with low education. In addition, the FN is an alternative for those who are dissatisfied with France's political system.

Equally importantly, and in addition to the fact that the FN has done better in the countryside than in cities, the FN electorate has become younger under Marine Le Pen. This shift in support patterns may be explained by two phenomena. Internally, with the election of Marine Le Pen, the party has become younger, more dynamic, and more appealing to a young electorate. Externally, it is the young who are suffering the brunt of the economic crisis: they are nearly twice as likely to be unemployed, they struggle to find good jobs, and they lack connections to the mainstream parties, which are frequently perceived as elitist and out of touch with the problems of the young generation. In such a situation, the young generation might look for an alternative with a different programme and agenda. It could well be that the FN is that party.

What do the results from this analysis tell us about the future electoral prospects of the FN? Most importantly, they tell us that the party has not managed to become the catch-all party that it has aspired to become. Rather, except for its success among young adults, the FN electorate is still largely composed of individuals who have been traditionally inclined to support the radical right. Hence, I predict that the FN will not succeed in making further electoral gains. This applies even more if we consider that the electoral base of the party is declining rather than growing. In a highly industrialized country such as France, it is highly unlikely that education levels are declining. The same applies to blue-collar jobs; this type of employment will rather wane than increase, despite FN calls for a reindustrialization of France. In addition, it is also likely that dissatisfaction levels with democracy will continue to dwindle. Between 2007, 1 year before the economic crisis started, and 2012, the 4th year of the ongoing crisis, satisfaction levels with democracy barely dropped. Therefore, it is improbable that they will drop further; this applies even more if we

6.5 Discussion

consider that France might return to economic growth (for 2015 the economic growth prospects are 1.8 %; see European Commission 2015). However, an economy that recovers slowly might not mean that satisfaction levels with President Hollande, the socialist government, and the main moderate right-wing alternative the Republicans, will increase. If this is the case, frustration with the main parties might still push voters to support the FN electorally.

In addition, despite the fact that a majority of the French public now considers the FN a party like others, I also deem it very improbable that the FN alternative programme will become mainstream. The FN is a party that operates at the—albeit broad—fringes of the system, and it will continue to do so. The majority of the French population will not support an alternative to the current democratic order. In contrast, what could play in the FN's favour is its recent tendency to disproportionately attract young voters. The party could profit in two ways. First, young voters are probably the easiest to convince to vote FN, because they do not have set party ideologies and as a group they are in a very unstable situation. Considering the large percentage of non-voters among those under 35 years of age, there is also a large potential for the FN under Marine Le Pen to further increase this vote base. Second, and even more importantly for the party, is the possibility that these "new" voters will become habitual FN voters. In this case, the FN might develop new cohorts of faithful voters. However, it is still too early to determine whether or not this generational effect will become a reality.

Chapter 7
Conclusion

Since Marine Le Pen took over the presidency from Jean-Marie Le Pen, in 2011, the FN has advanced faster and further than any other time in its 40-year history. The party has never been more beneficially treated by the media; about half of the French population perceive the FN as a normal party, as a party like others. Public support and voter intentions in favour of the FN president have reached upwards of 30 % of the population. When it comes to membership, the party has never been stronger, and in terms of electoral support, the FN is now the preferred choice of one-fourth of the French electorate. How has this unprecedented boost in positive opinion, membership figures, and votes been possible? How did the FN climb to these new heights? What actually changed between Jean-Marie Le Pen and Marine Le Pen?

Using a supply-and-demand framework, I set out to answer these questions in this book. I started the discussion of the FN with the premise that Marine Le Pen has had a tremendous opportunity to succeed. In the second decade of the twenty-first century, France has faced three crises, all of which have benefited an anti-system party such as the FN. First, there is the economic crisis with high unemployment and soaring debt. This crisis has crippled France for over half a dozen years and continues to linger as of 2015. Second, there is a political crisis characterized by the delegitimization of the mainstream elites. Shaken by personal and political turmoil and seen as incapable of solving the pressing economic and social problems of the twenty-first century, the French president, François Hollande, and his Socialist Party have been at record lows in public opinion for some time now. The centre-left's main contender, the Republicans have scored only slightly better, if at all. Divided in leadership and programme, the former UMP has not been able to elevate itself as a credible and cherished alternative to the PS in public opinion, leaving a good deal of room for the FN to flourish. To this political crisis at home is added a crisis of governance at the European level; the debt and refugee crises—to name two challenges—are far from being resolved. Third, a latent cultural and identity crisis with growing fears over an overpopulation of France by Muslims is perceptible in France (Mavelli 2014).

However, these crises alone cannot explain why the FN has taken off on all fronts. Rather than depending on a favourable structural environment, to a great extent, the success of a party such as the FN depends on agency: the capacity to place its message, create demand for its platform, and respond to latent demand for action within the population (Stockemer 2013: 20). I argue that through some changes in Marine Le Pen's leadership style and through a rhetorical, rather than substantive, renewal of its programme and ideology, the FN benefited prodigiously from tremendous structural opportunities that opened up in past years. The FN's anti-system, anti-elite, anti-globalization, anti-European message resonates well within a political landscape rattled by crises; this is even truer considering that the FN and its leader have presented the party's traditional message within a republican framework.

Since taking the reins of the party, Marine Le Pen has always claimed that the FN is a republican party; she has stressed republican concepts (such as sovereignty and *laïcité*), even if these concepts are used either to denounce Europe or the European Union or to attack Islam. Equally importantly, Marine Le Pen has completely stopped the anti-Jewish jokes and discourses, which were a regular part of her father's speeches. As part of her deradicalization strategy, Marine Le Pen has also normalized her relationship with the media. Media outlets and their representatives are seen no longer as inherently evil but as an ally, which the FN needs to further push its message. While remaining faithful to its ethno-centric, nationalistic, and more authoritarian framework, Marine Le Pen and the party leadership have further refined the party's economic platform and the presentation of the party's main theses. Marine Le Pen has accelerated and completed the economic reorientation of FN towards left-wing ideals, something Jean-Marie Le Pen started more than a decade ago. Economically, Marine Le Pen has now firmly situated her party within the left, by giving the FN a left-wing socialistic program, albeit with a nationalist component. The targeted constituencies of this renewed thematic focus are the working classes.

So how have these reforms, which have not tackled the core of the FN program, played out? Through an analysis of the members and voters, I have shown that the FN's deradicalization strategy has worked; the FN is no longer the devil at the fringes. Rather, when it comes to membership it has become a catch-all party. The party's members come from all backgrounds, genders, ages, and social and political classes. Whether they have been socialized into a radical right-wing milieu, whether they have been frustrated by the centre-right or even leftist parties and groups, whether they have joined the party due to some concrete or formative event, whether they have college, high school, or university education, and whether they are negatively influenced by immigration, social disruption, or European integration, the uniting force for all FN members is nationalistic sentiment. FN members and voters are fearful that their country might lose more of its sovereignty, that their nation might be submerged under foreigners and illegal immigrants, and that France might be ruined by its corrupt elites.

The swelling and of its membership to 80,000 and the accompanying diversification indicate that the FN's ideas can spread to a wide variety of individuals, if presented in the "right" way at the "right" time by the "right" person. As such, the analysis of the FN members has shown that the FN ideas can become appealing within all strata of the French population, albeit only to individuals. In contrast, the evaluation of FN voters shows that the FN's message has not resonated to equal degrees within the population at large. Rather, the FN's target audience—the popular strata and individuals with low education—are the most receptive to the FN's message. These cohorts of the population were overrepresented in the FN vote in 2012. Opinion polls conducted in 2014 confirm these results. For example, post-election polling indicates that 43 % of blue-collar workers, 38 % of individuals with low education, and 37 % of the unemployed voted for the FN in the 2014 European parliamentary elections (IPSOS 2014). In addition and in conformity with its role as an anti-system party, the FN under Marine Le Pen has continued to be particularly successful among individuals who are dissatisfied with how democracy works in France. However, the only really new group that the FN opened up for itself are young voters. More than any other cohort, individuals aged 18–34 were overrepresented in the FN vote in 2012 and probably thereafter.

Quo vadis FN? This is the question that I want to answer on the final pages of this book. It is certain that by taking advantage of a favourable opportunity structure, the FN has carved out a larger political space for itself. With little programmatic change, but smart leadership and a repackaging of its message, the FN has created a seismic shift in French politics, which various authors have called a "tsunami" and a "tidal wave" (Oliveau 2014; Jaxel-Truer and Wieder 2014). Can the party sustain its current growth? Can it continue to ride this wave of success? Can it grow further in terms of both membership and electoral results? Despite its impressive results, I am rather sceptical and think that there are at least six potential hurdles or roadblocks that may prove too great for the FN to surmount.

First, although it is true that the FN has made large gains in public opinion in membership and electoral success, it is also true that 50 % of the population still do not see the FN as a party like others. Even for a significant portion of members the FN is not a party like others; they prefer to keep their engagement secret. Moreover, officially declaring one's FN party affiliation can still trigger negative societal reactions and discrimination. In addition, members are hesitant to put their name on FN lists. The future will show if the FN can get rid of these stigma, but this would probably entail a large programmatic overhaul of its ideology, something the FN and its leader are unable and unwilling to do.

Second, the FN is not a catch-all party in terms of voters; rather, the electoral pool that it can fish in is still rather limited, restricted mainly to individuals with low education, workers, and dissatisfied individuals. These cohorts will likely not grow in the population. Education levels in France will increase rather than decrease in the years and decades to come, the number of low-skilled and blue-collar jobs will decline rather than increase, and individuals' dissatisfaction with democracy will likely not drop further. This applies even more considering that the political class can hardly do worse than it has done over the past years. In addition, economic growth seems to have finally returned to France. Yet, the fact that it is overrepresented among young voters might play in the party's favour, in particular. If Marine

Le Pen manages to convince more young people to vote for the FN and if these young voters become habitual FN voters, then the FN future in terms of electoral success might continue to look promising. However, it is still too early to predict the long-term youth vote.

Third, there are inherent contradictions in the FN's programme. As Shields (2015) points out, there is a structural divide in the FN's agenda. On the social and moral side, its programme and ideology are characterized by authoritarian, nationalistic, and socially conservative values. On the economic side, it preaches an interventionist state and welfare chauvinism, which it considers attractive to a working-class electorate. However, these two elements are not necessarily compatible. Traditional rural supporters from the petit bourgeoisie might be attracted by the social component of the FN programme, but not necessarily by the economic component. In contrast, individuals with a decidedly left-wing ideology might be attracted by the FN's economic program but might shy away from the party's social proposals. In the current situation, these contradictions are hidden behind a crisis rhetoric, but once the various crises that France is currently suffering from wane, the contradictory nature of the FN's programme will probably resurface, to its detriment.

Fourth, despite the Front's rhetorical reinvention, it remains a radical party. Many of its propositions are still too extreme for conservative individuals, the main target of its social platform. For example, although 85 % of centre-right supporters favour the introduction of stronger punishment for petty crimes, only 23 % favour the restoration of the death penalty. Similarly, 63 % of UMP supporters favour the defence of traditional values, yet only 18 % support the FN's key policy proposal to withdraw from the euro and reintroduce the Franc (TNS Sofres 2015). Again, in order to attract more (mainstream) support, the FN would have to change its programme, something that is very unlikely to happen.

Fifth, the FN lacks potential political allies and representation. It has hardly any governing experience and starkly lacks representation. Specifically, the FN gained 25.2 % of the vote in the first round of the departmental elections and 22.5 % in the second round. This looks impressive, but it is less so when we look at how these votes translated into seats. Not only did the vote share drop from the first to the second round, but, even more important, it seems that the FN has no winning formula. It qualified for 1107 runoff elections in cantons, including 307 run-offs in which it won the first round. However, in the second round, it won only 25, or less than 4 %, of these run-off elections, confirming its position as a marginal force in representation (Shields 2015). A similar scenario occurred in the December 2015 regional elections: despite being the top party in the first round, despite winning some regions with a 10 % margin, the FN could not capitalize on these successes and did not win any regions in the second round.

Sixth, the FN is not a modern party. Despite efforts to professionalize the party and despite considerable human resources, the FN has archaic structures, which are hardly conceivable for a governing party. Marine Le Pen is the party's absolute leader. Not only does she appoint her faithful and, especially, her family friends to important party positions, but she runs the party with an iron fist. Anybody who opposes her or the official doctrine is either threatened with expulsion or actually

7 Conclusion

expelled. Despite all the admiration and the personality cult around her name, the literature on autocratic survival tells us that being a personalist autocrat is not without its dangers. If the autocrat cannot satisfy his or her followers, members of the elite may start to look for an alternative (Geddes 1999; Svolik 2012). This happened to Jean-Marie Le Pen in the late 1990s, when he was challenged personally and thematically by Bruno Mégret in what was the greatest leadership crisis to date. What happened to Jean-Marie Le Pen could also happen to Marine Le Pen. Ironically, Jean-Marie Le Pen recently attacked Marine Le Pen's leadership. Although this challenge has not hurt her—yet—it is far from clear that similar attacks either by Jean-Marie Le Pen or by somebody else might not hurt her in the future.

All this is not to say that the FN might not remain influential. In particular, if the multiple crises continue to linger, Marine Le Pen and her party will continue to find an environment propitious to prospering. In particular, if the structural environment remains beneficial, it is likely that the FN will continue to play a major role in French politics. The current refugee crisis, with hundreds of thousands of refugees reaching the shores of the European Union, might give the FN further pretext not only to instrumentalize its immigration leitmotif but also to recruit followers. Nevertheless, I predict that even if the structural environment remains beneficial, the FN's boost in public opinion, membership numbers, and election results is going to plateau (see also Crépon et al. 2015). In its current composition, the FN has likely reached out to as many people as it can. In particular in electoral terms, it will be unlikely to broaden its appeal, beyond the current success. However, this is not to say that 80,000 members and 25 % of the vote are unimpressive for a party that was, is, and will probably remain a party at the fringes of the French political system.

Appendix A: The Interviews

Interview 1 conducted on January 7, 2013 in La Défense
Interview 2 conducted on January 7, 2013 in La Défense
Interview 3 conducted on January 8, 2013 in Clichy
Interview 4 conducted on January 9, 2013 in Paris
Interview 5 conducted on January 15, 2013 in Paris
Interview 6 conducted on January 17, 2013 in Sevres
Interview 7 conducted on January 17, 2013 in Sevres
Interview 8 conducted on January 18, 2013 in Asnières sur Seine
Interview 9 conducted on January 21, 2013 in Paris
Interview 10 conducted on January 24, 2013 in Paris
Interview 11 conducted on January 27, 2013 in Puteaux
Interview 12 conducted on January 27, 2013 in Puteaux
Interview 13 conducted on January 28, 2013 in Paris
Interview 14 conducted on January 29, 2013 in Paris
Interview 15 conducted on January 31, 2013 in Paris
Interview 16 conducted on February 2, 2013 in Boulogne
Interview 17 conducted on February 2, 2013 in Boulogne
Interview 18 conducted on February 4, 2013 in Paris
Interview 19 conducted on February 15, 2013 in Paris
Interview 20 conducted on March 3, 2013 in Paris
Interview 21 conducted on March 3, 2013 in Paris
Interview 22 conducted on March 15, 2013 in Paris
Interview 23 conducted on March 29, 2013 in Paris
Interview 24 conducted on April 18, 2013 in Tours
Interview 25 conducted on April 27, 2013 in Nancy
Interview 26 conducted on April 27, 2013 in Nancy
Interview 27 conducted on May 7, 2013 in Grenoble
Interview 28 conducted on May 7, 2013 in Grenoble
Interview 29 conducted on May 7, 2013 in Grenoble
Interview 30 conducted on May 7, 2013 in Grenoble

Interview 31 conducted on May 15, 2013 in Tours
Interview 32 conducted on May 15, 2013 in Tours
Interview 33 conducted on May 15, 2013 in Tours
Interview 34 conducted on May 21, 2013 in St. Etienne
Interview 35 conducted on May 24, 2013 in Nantes
Interview 36 conducted on May 24, 2013 in Nantes
Interview 37 conducted on May 25, 2013 in Nantes
Interview 38 conducted on June 7, 2013 in Chalons
Interview 39 conducted on June 7, 2013 in Chalons
Interview 40 conducted on June 7, 2013 in Chalons
Interview 41 conducted on June 7, 2013 in Chalons
Interview 42 conducted on June 7, 2013 in Chalons
Interview 43 conducted on June 7, 2013 in Chalons
Interview 44 conducted on June 7, 2013 in Chalons

References

Adler, Patricia A., and Peter Adler. 1987. *Membership roles in field research*. Newbury Park, CA: Sage.
Adorno, Theodore W., Else Frenkel-Brunswik, Daniel J. Levinson, R. Nevitt Sanford, Betty Aron, Maria Hertz Levinson, and William Morrow. 1950. *The authoritarian personality*. New York: Harper and Row.
Albertini, Dominique, and David Doucet. 2013. *Histoire du front national*. Paris: Tallandier.
Alduy, Cécile, and Stéphane Wahnich. 2015. *Marine Le Pen prise aux mots: Décryptage du nouveau discours frontiste*. Paris: Seuil.
Aliot, Louis. 2013. Billet-dete-n5. http://www.frontnational.com/2013/08/billet-dete-n5/. Accessed 19 Oct 2013.
Almeida, Dimitri. 2013. Towards a post-radical Front National? Patterns of ideological change and dediabolisation on the French radical right. *Nottingham French Studies* 52(2): 167–176.
Aminzade, Ronald. 1993. Class analysis, politics, and French labor history. In *Rethinking labor history*, ed. Larry Berlanstein, 90–113. Urbana and Chicago: University of Illinois Press.
Arnautu, Marie Christine. 2015. Site officiel de Marie-Christine Arnautu, député au Parlement européen, conseiller Municipal de Nice et Vice-présidente du FN. arnoutu.fr. Accessed 9 July 2015.
Arnold Edward, J. 2000. *The development of the radical right in France: From boulanger to Le Pen*. London: Macmillan Press.
Art, David. 2011. *Inside the radical right: The development of anti-immigrant parties in Western Europe*. Cambridge: Cambridge University Press.
Arzheimer, K., and E. Carter. 2009. Christian religiosity and voting for West European radical right parties. *West European Politics* 32(5): 985–1011.
Arzheimer, K. 2012. Electoral sociology: Who votes for the extreme right and why—And when? In *The Extreme right in Europe. Current trends and perspectives*, eds. U. Backes, and P. Moreau. Göttingen: Vendenhoeck & Ruprecht.
Balent, Magali. 2012. *Le Monde Selon Marine: La Politique International du Front National*. Paris: Armand Colis.
Bariller, Damien, and Franck Timmermans. 1993. *20 ans au Front. L'histoire vraie du Front National (1972–1992)*. Paris: Éditions Nationales.
Barone, Sylvain and Emmanuel Négrier. 2015. Voter Front National en Milieu Rural: Une Perspective Ethnographique. In *Les Faux-Semblant Du Front National: Sociologie d'Un Parti Politique*, eds. Sylvain Crépon, Alexandré Dézé and Nonna Mayer, 417–434. Paris: Sciences Po Les Presses.
BBC News. 2014. French far-right 'at gates of power'—PM Manuel Valls. http://www.bbc.com/news/world-europe-29101128. Accessed 23 Aug 2015.

Beauzamy Brigitte. 2013. Explaining the rise of the Front National to electoral prominence: Multi-faceted or contradictory models? In *Right-wing populism in Europe: Politics and discourse*, eds. Ruth Wodak, Majid Khosravinik and Brigitte Mral, 177–189. London: Bloomsbury.

Bell, D.S. 1994. The French National Front. *History of European Ideas* 18(2): 225–240.

Berezin, Mabel. 2007. Revisiting the French National Front: The ontology of a political mood. *Journal of Contemporary Ethnography*. 36(2): 129–146.

Betz, Hans G. 2004. La droite populiste en Europe. Extrême et démocrate? *Pôle Sud* 21(2): 132–134.

Betz, Hans-G, and Stefan Immerfall. 1998. *The new politics of the right: Neo-populist parties and movements in established democracies*. London: MacMillan Press.

Birenbaum, Guy. 1992. *Le Front National en Politique*. Paris: Balland.

Birenbaum, Guy, Nonna Mayer and Pascal Perrineau. 1996. Le FN dans la durée. In *Le Front National à découvert*, eds. Nonna Mayer and Pascal Perrineau. Paris: Presses de Sciences Po.

Bizeul, Daniel. 2003. *Avec ceux du FN. Un sociologue au Front national*. Paris: La Découverte.

Bornschier, Simon. 2005. Unis contre la mondialisation? Une analyse de la convergence programmatique des partis populistes de droite européens. *Revue Internationale de Politique Comparée* 4(12): 415–432.

Bornschier, Simon, and Romain Lachat. 2009. The evolution of the French political space and party system. *West European Politics* 32(2): 360–383.

Bornschier, Simon. 2012. Why a right-wing populist party emerged in France but not in Germany: Cleavages and actors in the formation of a new cultural divide. *European Political Science Review* 4(1): 121–145.

Boulanger, Jean-Luis. 1990. *Le rendez-vous manqué de la rénovation*. Paris: Seuil.

Bourseiller, Christophe. 1991. *Extrême Droite. L'Enquête*. Paris: François Bourin.

Bremner, Charles. 2014. At the gates of power: How Marine Le Pen is unnerving the French establishment. The New Statesman (December 2, 2014) News post. http://www.newstatesman.com/politics/2014/12/gates-power-how-marine-le-pen-unnerving-french-establishment. Accessed 7 Oct 2016.

Bresson, Gilles, and Christian Lionet. 1994. *Le Pen: biographie*. Paris: Éditions du Seuil.

Bussi, M., and J. Fourquet. 2007. Élection présidentielle 2007 Neuf cartes pour comprendre. *Revue française de science politique* 57(3): 411–428.

Bussi, M., J. Fourquet, and C. Colange. 2012. Analyse et compréhension du vote lors des élections présidentielles de 2012, l'apport de la géographie électorale. *Revue française de science politique* 62(5): 941–963.

Camus, Jean-Yves. 1996. Origine et formation du Front National. In *Le Front National à dé couvert*, eds. Nonna Mayer and Pascal Perrineau. Paris: Presses de Sciences Po.

———. 2011. Le FN est toujours un parti d'extrême droite. http://www.iris-france.org/44947-le-fn-est-toujours-un-parti-dextrme-droite/. Accessed 13 Aug 2015.

Charlot, Monica. 1986. L'émergence du Front National. *Revue Française de Science Politique* 36 (1): 30–45.

Clark, J.A., and J.S. Legge Jr. 1997. Economics, racism, and attitudes toward immigration in the new Germany. *Political Research Quarterly* 50(4): 901–917.

Cohen, Philippe, and Pierre Péan. 2012. *Le Pen une Histoire Française*. Paris: Robert Laffont.

Colombier, Matthieu. 2011. Union des patriotes face à la racaille. http://avaricum.unblog.fr/2011/06/06/union-des-patriotes-face-a-la-racaille/. Accessed 21 Sept 2013.

Coomarasamy, James. 2011, Oct 22. Marine Le Pen: Detoxifying France's national front. *BBC News*, Paris. file:///C:/Users/Hp/Desktop/Major%20Paper/News%20articles/BBC%20News%20-%20Marine%20Le%20Pen%20%20'Detoxifying'%20France's%20National%20Front.htm. Accessed 17 June 2013.

Copsey, Nathaniel. 1997. A comparison between the extreme right in contemporary France and Britain. *Contemporary European History* 6(1): 101–116.

Corbière, Alexis, and Pena-Ruiz Henri. 2012. *Le parti de l'étrangère Bruxelles*. Bruxelles: Éditions Tribord.

Crépon, Sylvain. 1999. *Les Logiques identitaires de l'idéologie des militants du Front national de la jeunesse, une perspective socio-anthropologique sur les nationalisme d'extrême droite des années 90*. Doctoral thesis, Université de Paris X-Nanterre.
———. 2006. *La nouvelle extrême droite – Enquête sur les jeunes militants du Front National*. Paris: L'Harmattan.
———. 2012. *Enquête au coeur du nouveau Front national*. Paris: Nouveau Monde.
Crépon, Sylvain, Alexandré Dézé, and Nonna Mayer. 2015. Quelles Perspectives pour le Front National. In *Les Faux-Semblant Du Front National: Sociologie d'Un Parti Politique*, eds. Sylvain Crépon, Alexandré Dézé and Nonna Mayer, 529–536. Paris: Presses des Sciences Po.
Davies, Phillip. 1999. *The National Front and France: Ideology, discourses, and power*. New York: Routledge.
De Lange, Sarah L. 2007. A new winning formula? The programmatic appeal of the radical right. *Party Politics* 13(4): 411–435.
DeClair, Edward G. 1999. *Politics on the fringe: The people, policies, and organization of the French National Front*. Durham: Duke University Press Books.
Dézé, Alexandre. 2012. *Le Front national: à la conquête du pouvoir?* Paris: Armand Colin.
———. 2015. La Dédiabolisation: Une Nouvelle Stratégie. In *Les Faux-Semblant Du Front National: Sociologie d'Un Parti Politique*, eds. Sylvain Crépon, Alexandré Dézé and Nonna Mayer, 27–45. Paris: Presses des Sciences Po.
Eatwell, Roger. 2000. The rebirth of the extreme right in Western Europe. *Parliamentary Affairs* 53(3): 407–425.
Engelmann, Fabien. 2014. Enlèvement d'une jeune femme de 22 ans à Hayange: stop au laxisme de la justice. http://www.frontnational.com/2014/08/enlevement-dune-jeune-femme-de-22-ans-a-hayange-stop-au-laxisme-de-la-justice/. Accessed 21 Oct.
Euroactiv. 2014. Marine Le Pen loses immunity as MEP in racism case. http://www.euractiv.com/justice/marine-le-pen-loses-immunity-mep-news-529044. Accessed 21 Jan 2014.
European Commission. 2015. European economic forecast: Winter 2015. http://ec.europa.eu/economy_finance/publications /european_economy/2015/ pdf/ee1_en.pdf. Accessed 2 June 2015.
Evans, Jocyline A., and Gilles Ivaldi. 2005. An extremist autarky: The systemic separation of the French extreme right. *Southern European Politics and Society* 10(2): 351–366.
Falter, Juergen W. 1983. Arbeitslosigkeit und Nationalsozialismus. Eine empirische Analyse des Beitrags der Massenarbeitslosigkeit zu den Wahlerfolgen der NSDAP 1932 und 1933. *Koelner Zeitschrift für Soziologie und Sozialpsychologie* 3(4): 525–554.
Falter, Juergen, and Sigfried Schumann. 1988. Affinity towards right-wing extremism in Western Europe. *West European Politics* 11(2): 96–110.
Favier, Pierre, and Michel Martin-Roland. 1990. *La Décennie de Mitterrand*. Paris: Seuil.
Fornilli, Véronique. 2013. Islam et République. http://www.fnjeunesse.fr/2013/04/12/1923/. Accessed 12 Oct 2013.
Freedman, J. 2004. *Immigration and insecurity in France*. Aldershot: Ashgate.
French Ministry of Interior. 2014. Résultats des élections européennes 2014. http://www.interieur.gouv.fr/Elections/Les-resultats/Europeennes/elecresult__ER2014/%28path%29/ER2014/index.html. Accessed 5 Oct 2014.
Frey, Hugo. 1998. Questions of decolonization and post-colonialism in the ideology of the French extreme right. *European Studies* 28(1): 69–88.
Gauthier, Jean-Pierre. 2009. *Les extremes droites en France: De la traverse du désert à l'ascension du Front National (1945–2008)*. Paris: Éditions Syllepse.
Geddes, Barbara. 1999. What do we know about democratization after twenty years? *Annual Review of Political Science* 2: 115–144.
Givens, T. 2004. The radical right gender gap. *Comparative Political Studies* 37(1): 30–54.
Gollnisch, Bruno. 2013. Contre le racism à sens unique. http://www.frontnational.com/2013/07/contre-le-racisme-a-sens-unique/. Accessed 2 Oct 2014.

---. 2015. Historique des Legislatures. http://www.europarl.europa.eu/meps/fr/1164/BRUNO_GOLLNISCH_history.html. Accessed 4 Aug.
Goodwin, R., P. Costa, and J. Adonu. 2004. Social support and its consequences: 'Positive' and 'deficiency' values and their implications for support and self-esteem. *British Journal of Social Psychology* 43: 465–474.
Goodliffe, Gabriel. 2012. *The resurgence of the National Front in France: From boulangisme to the Front National.* Cambridge: Cambridge University Press.
Goodwin, Jeff. 2001. Introduction: Why emotions matter. In *Passionate politic: Emotions and social movements,* eds. Jeff Goodwin, James M. Jasper and Francesca Poletta, 1–24. Cambridge: Cambridge University Press.
Goodwin, Jeff, and James M. Jasper. 2004. Caught in winding, snarling vine: The structural bias of political process theory. In *Rethining social movements' structure, meaning and emotions,* eds. Jeff Goodwin and James M. Jasper, 3–32. Lanham: Rowman & Littlefield.
Goodwin, Matthew, Robert Ford, and David Cutts. 2012. Extreme right foot soldiers, legacy effects and deprivation: A contextual analysis of the leaked British National Party (BNP) membership list. *Party Politics* 19(6): 887–906.
Gougou, Florent. 2015. Les Ouvriers et le Vote Front National: Les Logiques d'un Réalignement Électoral. In *Les Faux-Semblant Du Front National: Sociologie d'Un Parti Politique,* eds. Sylvain Crépon, Alexandré Dézé and Nonna Mayer, 323–342. Paris: Presses des Sciences Po.
Guest, Greg, Arwen Bunce, and Laura Johnson. 2006. How many interviews are enough?: An experiment with data saturation and variability. *Field Methods* 18(1): 59–82.
Hainsworth, Paul. 2000. *The politics of the extreme right: From margins to the mainstream.* London: Pinter.
---. 2004. The rise and rise of Jean Marie Le Pen's front national. *Representation* 40(2): 101–114.
---. 2008. *The extreme right in Western Europe.* New York: Routledge.
Hainsworth, Paul, and Paul Mitchell. 2000. France: The Front National from crossroads to crossroads? *Parliamentary Affairs* 53(3): 443–456.
Hameau, C. 1992. *La campagne de Jean-Marie Le Pen pour l'élection présidentielle de 1988.* Paris: L.G.D.J.
Hewlett, Mark. 2012. Voting in the shadow of the crisis. The French presidential and parliamentary elections of 2012. *Modern and Contemporary France* 20(4): 403–420.
Hooghe, Lisbet, Gary Marks, and Carole J. Wilson. 2002. Does left/right structure party positions on European integration. *Comparative Political Studies* 35(8): 965–989.
Huffington Post. 2015. Jean-Marie Le Pen gagne son procès contre le FN après sa suspension. http://www.huffingtonpost.fr/2015/07/02/jean-marie-le-pen-fn-gagne-proces-contre-fn-apres-suspension_n_7712610.html. Accessed 23 Aug.
Huntington, Samuel P. 1996. *The clash of civilizations and the remaking of world order.* New York: Simon & Schuster.
Ifop sondages. 2015. Les Français et la candidature de François Hollande en 2017. http://www.youscribe.com/catalogue/tous/actualite-et-debat-de-societe/politique/sondage-2650686. Accessed 15 Sept 2015.
Ignazi, Piero. 2003. *Extreme right parties in Western Europe.* New York: Oxford University Press.
---. 2013. Le Front National et les autres. Influence et évolutions. In *Le Front National. Mutations de l'extrême droite française,* ed. Pascal Delwit, 57–76. Bruxelles: Éditions de l'Université de Bruxelles.
Igounet, Valérie 2014. *Le Front national de 1972 à nos Jours: le Parti, les Hommes, les IdÉes.* Paris: Éditions du Seuil.
Immerzeel, T., E. Jaspers, and M. Lubbers. 2013. Religion as catalyst or restraint of radical right voting? *West European Politics* 36(5): 946–968.
IPSOS. 2014. Elections européennes 2014—comprendre le vote des Français. http://www.ipsos.fr/sites/default/files/attachments/europeennes_ipsos_-_comprendre_le_vote_des_francais_-_25_mai_2014_-_20h.pdf. Accessed 2 Sept 2015.

References

Ivaldi, Gilles. 1998. The Front National: The making of an authoritarian party. In *The organisation of political parties in Southern Europe*, eds. Piero Ignazi and Colette Gmail. Westport, CT: Praeger Publisher.
———. 2015. Towards the median economic crisis voter? The new leftist economic agenda of the Front National in France. *French Politics* 13(4): 346–369.
Jamet, France. 2012. Aude/Carcassonne – Les Français ne sont pas les bienvenus à La Conte. http://www.francejamet.fr/?cat=1&paged=6. Accessed 21 Sept 2014.
Jaxel-Truer, Pierre, and Thomas Wieder. 2014. Le séisme qui ébranle la vie politique française. http://www.lemonde.fr/politique/article/2014/05/26/europeennes-le-seisme-qui-ebranle-la-vie-politique-francaise_4425980_823448.html. Accessed 3 Sept 2015.
Jennings, M. Kent, and Richard Niemi. 1981. *Generations in politics*. Princeton: Princeton University Press.
Jouve, Pierre, and Ali Magoudi. 1988. *Les dits et les non-dits de Jean-Marie Le Pen: enquêtes et psychanalyse*. Paris: La DÉcouverte.
Kessler, Alan E., and Gary P. Freeman. 2005. Public opinion in the EU on immigration from outside the community. *Common Market Studies* 43(4): 825–850.
Kitschelt, Herbert. 1995. *The radical right in Western Europe: A comparative analysis*. Ann Arbor, MI: University of Michigan Press.
———. 2007. Growth and persistence of the radical right in postindustrial democracies: Advances and challenges in comparative research. *West European Politics* 30(5): 1176–1206.
Klandermans, Bert. 1986. Psychology and trade union participation: Joining, acting, and quitting. *Journal of Occupational Psychology* 59(3): 189–204.
———. 1997. *The social psychology of protest*. Cambridge: Blackwell.
———. 2004. The demand and supply of participation: Social psychological correlates of participation in social movements. In *The Blackwell companion of social movements*, eds. David A. Snow, Sarah A. Soule and Hans-Peter Kriesi. Oxford: Blackwell.
———. 2013. Extreme right activists: Recruitment and experiences. In *Right wind radicalism today. Perspectives from Europe and the US*, eds. Sabine Von Mering and Timothy W. McCarty, 60–84. London: Routedge.
Klandermans, Bert, and Nonna Mayer, eds. 2006. *Extreme right activists in Europe: Through the magnifying glass*. London: Routledge.
Kling, Anne. 2012. *FN...Tout ça pour ça! La très étonnante évolution du Front National*. Strasbourg: Éditions Mithra.
Krastev, Ivan. 2007. Is East-Central Europe backsliding? The strange death of the liberal consensus. *Journal of Democracy* 18(4): 56–63.
Kriesi, Hanspeter, Edgar Grande, Romain Lachat, Martin Dolezal, Simon Bornschier, and Timotheos Frey. 2008. *West European politics in the age of globalization*. Cambridge: Cambridge University Press.
L'Express. 2014. Jean-Marie Le Pen est-il vraiment un boulot. http://www.lexpress.fr/actualite/politique/fn/jean-marie-le-pen-est-il-vraiment-un-boulet_1615308.html. Accessed 1 Nov 2014.
———. 2015. Jean Marie Le Pen exclu du FN. http://www.lexpress.fr/actualite/politique/fn/jean-marie-le-pen-suspendu-du-fn_1677175.html. Accessed 5 March 2016.
La Libération. 2013. Marine Le Pen s'insurge contre l'étiquette "extrême droite" du FN. http://www.liberation.fr/politiques/2013/10/02/marine-le-pen-s-insurge-contre-l-etiquette-extreme-droite-du-fn_936353. Accessed 21 Oct 2014.
———. 2015. Conflit au FN: Le rapport de force reste favorable à Marine Le Pen. http://www.liberation.fr/politiques/2015/07/09/conflit-au-fn-le-rapport-de-force-reste-favorable-a-marine-le-pen_1345330. Accessed 31 Aug.
Lafont, Valerie. 2001. Les jeunes militants du Front national: trois modèles d'engagement et de cheminement. *Revue Française de Sciences Politique* 51(1–2): 175–198.
Laubacher, Paul. 2014. Municipales: les trois victoires du Front National. *Le Nouvel Observateur*. http://tempsreel.nouvelobs.com/elections-municipales-2014/20140330.OBS1903/municipales-les-trois-victoires-du-front-national.html. Accessed 22 Oct 2014.

Le Bohec, Jacques. 2005. *Sociologie du phénomène Le Pen*. Paris: DÉcouverte.
Le Figaro. 2013. Le FN, un parti comme les autres pour 54 pourcent des Français. http://www.itele.fr/politique/video/le-fn-un-parti-comme-les-autres-pour-54-des-francais-55195.
———. 2014. Le FN aurait doublé son nombre d'adhérents depuis 2012. http://www.lefigaro.fr/politique/le-scan/coulisses/2014/10/31/25006-20141031ARTFIG00061-le-fn-aurait-double-son-nombre-d-adherents-depuis-2012.php?pagination=14. Accessed 3 Nov 2014.
———. 2015. Le Pen en tête des intentions de vote. http://www.lefigaro.fr/flash-actu/2015/01/29/97001-20150129FILWWW00194-le-pen-en-tete-des-intentions-de-vote.php. Accessed 31 July 2015.
LeCoeur, Erwan, and Enzo Poultreniez. 2013. *Face au FN*. Paris: Repères contre le racisme, pour la diversité et la solidarité internationale.
Le Front National. 2006. Programme Fraternité – Emploi. http://www.frontnational.com/doc_frater_emploi.php. Accessed 4 April 2006.
———. 2007. Élection Présidentielle 2007: Programme. http://ipolitique.free.fr/francepolitique/lepen2007.pdf. Accessed 5 Oct 2014.
———. 2008a. 300 mesures pour la renaissance de la France. www.frontnational.com/doc_id_immigration.php. Accessed 17 March 2008.
———. 2008b. Sécurité et Justice. http://frontnational.com/programmesecurite. Accessed 17 March 2008.
———. 2008c. Sécurité Sociale. http://frontnational.com/programmesecu.php. Accessed 17 March 2008.
———. 2012. Le Projet du Front National. http://www.frontnational.com/le-projet-de-marine-le-pen/. Accessed 21 March 2015.
———. 2013a. Réaction du Front National à la levée de l'immunité parlementaire de Marine Le Pen. http://www.frontnational.com/2013/07/reaction-du-front-national-a-la-levee-de-limmunite-parlementaire-de-marine-le-pen/. Accessed 23 Oct 2013.
———. 2013b. Gilbert Collard interpelle le gouvernement sur la situation d'insécurité de la ZUS de Saint-Pierre-du-Mont. http://www.frontnational.com/2013/10/gilbert-collard-interpelle-le-gouvernement-sur-la-situation-dinsecurite-de-la-zus-de-saint-pierre-du-mont/. Accessed 27 Oct 2014.
———. 2013c. Intervention de Marion Marechal Le Pen sur le mariage homosexuel. http://www.frontnational.com/videos/intervention-de-marion-marechal-le-pen-sur-le-mariage-homosexuel/.
Le Front National 81. 2011. En avant pour la révolution patriotique: La tournée de France Jamet en pays d'Oc. http://frontnational81.over-blog.com/article-en-avant-pour-la-revolution-patriotique-65722763.html. Accessed 21 Sept 2014.
Le Front National Alpes-Maritimes. 2013. Tribune de Julien Glos. http://www.fn06.net/tribune-de-julien-clos. Accessed 20 Sept 2014.
Le Front National de l'Indre. 2013. Le Front National de l'Indre: Défendons nos couleurs. http://frontnat36.hautetfort.com/tag/immigration. Accessed 29 Oct 2014.
Le Front National de la Jeunesse. 2011. Pas de racaille dans nos quartiers. http://faj.hautetfort.com/archive/2010/12/21/nouvel-autocolant-faj-pas-de-racaille-dans-nos-quartiers.html. Accessed 21 Sept 2013.
———. 2013a. Nos Valeurs. http://www.fnjeunesse.fr/charte/nos-valeurs/. Accessed 12 Nov 2013.
———. 2014. Retour the Nicolas à Toulouse: Les Jeunes avec Marine lui disent Merci. http://www.fnjeunesse.fr/2014/10/09/retour-de-nicolas-a-toulouse-les-jeunes-avec-marine-lui-disent-merci/. Accessed 14 Oct 2014.
Le Front National de la Jeunesse en Alpes Maritimes. 2013. Encore de l'inscurité, toujours de l'insécurité. http://fn66.fr/tag/insecurite/. Accessed 23 Sept 2014.
Le Front National Loire. 2014. Le ramadan arrêtons la compassion. http://www.frontnational86.fr/les-journalistes-et-le-ramadan-arretons-la-compassion/. Accessed 30 Sept 2014.
Le Front National Loiret. 2014. L'islamisation du Loiret. http://www.fn-45.net/juin-septebre-2014/. Accessed 12 Oct 2014.

Le Front National Rhône. 2014. Maire de Lyon: je ne célèbrerai pas de marriage gay. http://www.fn69.fr/2013/06/maire-de-lyon-je-ne-celebrerai-pas-de-mariage-gay/. Accessed 23 Nov 2016.
Le Goff, J.P. 2011. Le syndrome du front national. *Le Débat* 166(4): 53–62.
Le Monde. 2014a. Le Front National: Parti d'extrême droite? http://www.lemonde.fr/idees/article/2013/10/04/le-front-national-parti-d-extreme-droite_3489871_3232.html. Accessed 12 Oct 2014.
———. 2014b. Marine Le Pen sur son père: l'avenir du FN, c'est moi et non pas lui. http://www.lemonde.fr/politique/article/2014/06/18/les-conseils-de-jean-marie-le-pen-a-sa-fille_4440209_823448.html.
———. 2014c. Dans l'Hérault, les Jamet, l'autre famille régnante du Front national. http://www.lemonde.fr/politique/article/2012/05/28/dans-l-herault-les-jamet-l-autre-famille-regnante-du-front-national_1708341_823448.html. Accessed 8 March 2014.
———. 2015. Marine Le Pen, jugée pour ses propos comparant prières de rue et Occupation, a été relaxée. *En savoir plus sur*. http://www.lemonde.fr/police-justice/article/2015/12/15/marine-le-pen-va-etre-fixee-sur-ses-propos-comparant-prieres-de-rue-et-occupation_4832052_1653578.html#OhUz9cjUXToxuSqs.99. Accessed 5 March 2016.
Le Nouvel Observateur. 2009. Les précédents dérapages de Jean-Marie Le Pen. http://tempsreel.nouvelobs.com/politique/20090325.OBS0618/les-precedents-derapages-de-jean-marie-le-pen.html. Accessed 2 Sept 2015.
Le Pen, Marine. 2014. Explosion de l'immigration clandestine: l'impératif retour aux frontières nationales. (Press release August 5th, 2014). http://www.frontnational.com/2014/08/explosion-de-limmigration-clandestine-limperatif-retour-aux-frontieres-nationales/. Accessed 23 Oct 2015.
Le Point. 2015. Le FN, un parti comme les autres, selon les Français. http://www.lepoint.fr/politique/le-fn-un-parti-comme-les-autres-selon-les-francais-30-01-2015-1901137_20.php. Accessed 13 June 2015.
Lebourg, Nicolas, and Joseph Beauregard. 2012. *Dans l'Ombre des Le Pen: une Histoire des Numéros 2 du FN*. Paris: Nouveau Monde Éditions.
Lecoeur, Erwan. 2003a. *Un Néo-Populisme à la française: Trente ans de Front National*. Paris: La découverte.
———. 2003b. L'inexorable ancrage du Front national. *L'Ecoren, Revue Critique de l'Écologie Politique*. http://ecorev.org/spip.php?article123. Accessed 20 March 2015.
———. 2007. *Dictionnaire de l'Extrême Droite*. Paris: Larousse.
Liang, Christina S., eds. 2007. *Europe for the Europeans: The foreign and security policy of the populist radical right*. Farnham: Ashgate.
Lichbach, Mark I. 1994. Rethinking rationality and rebellion: Theories of collective action and problems collective dissent. *Rationality and Society* 6(1): 8–39.
Loch, D., and W. Heitmeyer. 2001. *Schattenseiten der Globalisierung: Rechtsradikalismus, Rechtspopulismus und Regionalismus in Westeuropa*. Frankfurt am Main: Suhrkamp.
Lorien, Joseph, Karl Criton, and Serge Dumon. 1985. *Le Système Le Pen*. Antwerp: EPO.
Lucassen, Geertje, and M. Lubbers. 2012. Who fears what? Explaining far-right-wing preference in Europe by distinguishing perceived cultural and economic ethnic threats. *Comparative Political Studies* 45(5): 547–574.
Machuret, Patrice. 2012. *Dans la Peau de Marine Le Pen*. Paris: Seuil.
Marcilly, Jean, and Jean Marie Le Pen. 1984. *Le Pen sans Bandeau: 1928–1984*. Paris: Jacques Grancher.
Marcus, Jonathon. 1995. *The national front and French politics*. Basingstoke: Macmillan.
Maréchal, Samuel. 1994. *Ni droite ni gauche … Français! Contre la Pensée unique: l'autre Politique*. Paris: Première ligne.
Mathias, Bernard. 2007. Le Pen, Un Provocateur En Politique (1984–2002). *Vingtième Siècle Revue d'histoire* 93(1): 37–45.

Mavelli, Lucas. 2014. Europe's identity crisis, Islam in Europe, and the crisis of European secularity. In *Routledge handbook of Islam in the West*, ed. Roberto Tottoli. London: Routledge.
Mayer, Nonna. 1998. The Front National vote in the plural. *Patterns of Prejudice* 32(1): 3–24.
———. 2002. Les Hauts et les Bas du vote Le Pen. *Revue Française de Science politique* 52(5–6): 505–520.
———. 2007. Comment Nicolas Sarkozy a rétréci l'électorat Le Pen. *Revue française de science politique* 57(3): 429–445.
———. 2012. Le populisme est-il fatal? *Critique* 776–777: 141–149.
———. 2013. From Jean-Marie to Marine Le Pen: Electoral change on the far right. *Parliamentary Affairs* 66(1): 160–178.
———. 2015. The closing of the radical right gender gap in France? *French Politics* 13(4): 391–414.
McAdam, Doug. 1982. *Political process and the development of black insurgency, 1930–1980*. Chicago: University of Chicago Press.
———. 1988. *Freedom Summer*. New York: Oxford University Press.
Merkl, Peter H., and Leonard Weinberg. 1993. *Encounters with the contemporary radical right*. Oxford: Westview Press.
Milza, Pierre. 1987. *Fascisme français. Passé et Présent*. Paris: Flammarion.
Ministère de l'Intérieur. 2014. Résultats des élections européens 2014. http://www.interieur.gouv.fr/Elections/Les-resultats/Europeennes/elecresult__ER2014/(path)/ER2014/index.html. Accessed 23 Nov 2016.
———. 2015a. Les résultats. http://www.interieur.gouv.fr/Elections/Les-resultats. Accessed 21 Aug.
———. 2015b. Résultats des élections régionales 2015. http://www.interieur.gouv.fr/Elections/Les-resultats/Regionales/elecresult__regionales-2015/%28path%29/regionales-2015/index.html. Accessed 5 March 2016.
Minkenberg, Michael, and Pascal Perrineau. 2007. The radical right in the European elections 2004. *International Political Science Review* 28(1): 29–55.
Mondon, Aurelien. 2014. The Front National in the twenty-first century: From pariah to republican democratic contender? *Modern and Contemporary France* 22(3): 301–320.
Monnot, Caroline, and Abel Mestre. 2011. *Le système Le Pen: enquête sur les rÉseaux du Front National*. Paris: Denoël.
Mudde, Cas. 2010. The populist radical right: A pathological normalcy. *West European Politics* 33 (6): 1167–1186.
———. 2012. *The relationship between immigration and nativism in Europe and North America*. Washington, DC: Migration Policy Institute.
Mudde, Cas. 2013. Three decades of populist radical right parties in Western Europe: So what? *European Journal of Political Research* 52(81): 1–19.
New York Times. 2015. Jean Marie Le Pen, Co-founder of the national front, is ousted from French far right. http://www.nytimes.com/2015/08/21/world/europe/jean-marie-le-pen-france-national-front-party.html?_r=0. Accessed 9 March.
Oesch, D. 2008. Explaining workers' support for right-wing populist parties in Western Europe: Evidence from Austria, Belgium, France, Norway, and Switzerland. *International Political Science Review* 29(3): 349–373.
Oliveau, Thomas. 2014. 'Choc', 'séisme', 'big bang': les mots qui accompagnent la victoire du FN. http://www.lefigaro.fr/politique/le-scan/decryptages/2014/05/26/25003-20140526ARTFIG00187-choc-seisme-big-bang-ces-mots-qui-accompagnent-la-victoire-du-fn.php. Accessed 31 Aug 2015.
Orfali, Brigitta. 1991. *L'Adhésion au Front National – De la Minorité active au Mouvement Social*. Paris: Kimé.
Pasteau, Benoist. 2015. FN: Jean-Marie Le Pen "maintient" ses propos sur les chambres à gaz. http://www.europe1.fr/politique/jean-marie-le-pen-maintient-ses-propos-sur-les-chambre-a-gaz-2417203. Accessed 2 April.
Payne Stanely, G. 1996. *A history of fascism 1914–1945*. London: Routledge.

References

Pedahzur, Ami, and Avraham Brichta. 2002. The institutionalization of extreme right-wing charismatic parties: A paradox? *Party Politics* 8(1): 31–49.

Perrineau, Pascal. 1996. Le FN en 1995: une question de droite posée à la gauche. In *Aux Sources du Populisme Nationaliste: l'Urgence de comprendre Toulon, Orange, Marignane, La Tour d'Aigues*, ed. Jean Viard, 67–95. Paris: Éditions de L'Aube.

———. 1997. *Le Symptôme Le Pen: Radiographie des Electeurs du Front national*. Paris: Fayard, L'espace du politique.

———. 1998. Les étapes de l'implantation du Front national. In *L'Extrême Droite en France et en Belgique*, eds. Pascal Delwit, Jean-Michel De Waele and Andrea Rea, 29–55. Bruxelles: Édition Complexe.

———. 2012. La renaissance électorale de l'électorat frontiste. Élections 2012, les électorats politiques, note no 5. http://www.cevipof.com/fr/les-publications/notes-de-recherche/bdd/publication/966. Accessed 16 July 2015.

———. 2014. *La France au Front*. Paris: Fayard.

Pertusot, Vivien, and Yann-Sven Rittelmeyer. 2014. The European elections in France: The paradox of a more European yet more Eurosceptic campaign. EPIN Commentary No. 16. http://www.ceps.eu/book/european-elections-france-paradox-more-european-yet-more-eurosceptic-campaign. Accessed 18 Oct.

Phillipot, Florian. 2013. Engagement de la France en Syrie: Forian Philippot réagit sur iTélé. http://www.frontnational.com/videos/engagement-de-la-france-en-syrie-forian-philippot-reagit-sur-itele/. Accessed 2 Oct 2014.

———. 2014a. Prévisions budgétaires: Sapin dans la soumission absolute. http://www.frontnational.com/2014/09/previsions-budgetaires-sapin-dans-la-soumission-absolue/. Accessed 12 Oct 2014.

———. 2014b. Non-revalorisation des petites retraites: entre trahison et mépris du peuple. http://www.frontnational.com/2014/09/non-revalorisation-des-petites-retraites-entre-trahison-et-mepris-du-peuple/. Accessed 14 Oct 2014.

Quinn, Adrian. 2000. Tout est lié: The Front National and media conspiracy theories. *The Sociological Review* 48(2): 112–132.

Reynie, Dominique. 2011. Le tournant ethno-socialiste du Front national. *Études* 11(415): 463–472.

Rouban, L. 2013. Les électorats de Marine Le Pen ou les contraintes du succès. Élections 2014, Les enjeux, note no. 2. http://www.cevipof.com/fr/les-publications/notes-de-recherche/bdd/publication/1110. Accessed on 12 Oct 2015.

Roussel, Éric. 1985. *Le cas Le Pen – Les nouvelles Droites en France*. Paris: Jean-Claude Lattès.

Russo, Luana. 2014. France: The historic victory of the Front National. In *The European parliament elections of 2014*, eds. De Sio Lprenzo, Vincenco Emanuele and Nicola Maggini, 181–187, Rome: CISE.

Rydgren, Jens. 2004. *The populist challenge: Political protest and ethno-nationalist mobilization in France*. Oxford: Berghahn Books.

Rydgren, J., and P. Ruth. 2013. Contextual explanations of radical right-wing support in Sweden: Socioeconomic marginalization, group threat, and the halo effect. *Ethnic and Racial Studies* 36(4): 711–728.

Sargent, Lyman T. 1972. *Contemporary political ideologies: A comparative analysis*. Homewood: Dorsey Press.

Shields, James. 2007. *The extreme right in France: From Petain to Le Pen*. London: Routledge.

———. 2013. Marine Le Pen and the 'New' FN: A change of style or of substance? *Parliamentary Affairs* 66(1): 179–196.

———. 2015. The Front National at the polls: Transformational elections or the status quo reaffirmed? *French Politics* 13(4): 415–433.

Simmons, Harvey G. 2003. The French and European extreme right and globalization. Paper presented at the international seminar *Challenges to the New World Order: Anti-Globalism and Counter-Globalism*. Amsterdam, 30–31 May 2003.

Soudais, Michel. 1996. *Le Front National en Face*. Paris: Flammarion.

Startin, Nicolas. 2014. Contrasting fortunes, differing futures? The rise (and fall) of the Front National and the British National Party. *Modern and Contemporary France* 22(3): 277–299.
Stockemer, D. 2012. The Swiss radical right: Who are the (new) voters of the Swiss People's party. *Representation* 48(2): 197–208.
Stockemer, Daniel. 2013. *The micro and meso levels of activism: A comparative case study of Attac France and Attac Germany*. London: Palgrave McMillan.
———. 2014. Who are the members of the French Front National? Evidence from interview research. *French Politics* 12(1): 36–58.
Svolik, Milan. 2012. *The politics of authoritarian rule*. Cambridge: Cambridge University Press.
Taggart, Paul. 1995. New populist parties in Western Europe. *West European Politics* 18(1): 34–51.
Tiberj, V. 2012. La politique des deux axes: Variables sociologiques, valeurs et votes en France (1988–2007). *Revue française de science politique* 62(1): 71–106.
TNS Sofres. 2015. Baromètre d'image du front national. http://www.tns-sofres.com/sites/default/files/2015.02.16-baro-fn.pdf. Accessed 12 Sept 2015.
TNS-Sofres. 2012a. http://www.tns-sofres.com/_assets/files/2012.01.13-lepen.pdf. Accessed 12 Dec 2013.
———. 2012b. http://www.tns-sofres.com/_assets/files/2012.06.01-fn.pdf. Accessed 12 Dec 2013.
———. 2012c. http://www.tns-sofres.com/_assets/files/2012.01.12-barofn.pdf. Accessed 12 Dec 2013.
Tomz, Michael, Jason Wittenberg, and Gary King. 2003. Clarify: Software for interpreting and presenting statistical results. *Journal of Statistical Software* 8(1): 1–29.
Topido. 2014. Top 15 des pires citations de Jean-Marie Le Pen, celles qui donnent envie de changer de pays, de nationalité et de partir très très loin. http://www.topito.com/top-citations-jean-marie-le-pen-raciste-facho-borgne. Accessed 30 Oct 2015.
Van Der Brug, Wouter, Meindert Fennema, and Jean Tillie. 2005. Why some anti-immigrant parties fail and others succeed: A two-step model of aggregate electoral support. *Comparative Political Studies* 38(5): 537–573.
Van Dyke, Nella, and Marc Dixon. 2013. Activist human capital: Skills acquisition and the development of commitment to social movement activism. *Mobilization* 18(2): 197–212.
Van Stekelenburg, Jacqueline, and Bert Klandermans. 2007. Individuals in movements: A social psychology of contention. In *Handbook of social movements across disciplines*, eds. Bert Klandermans and Conny Roggeband, 157–204. London: Springer.
Vivas, Maxime and Frédéric Vivas. 2014. *Marine Le Pen amène le Pire*. Villeurbanne: Éditions Golias.
Von Mering, Sabine, and Timothy W. McCarty. 2013. *Right wind radicalism today. Perspectives from Europe and the US*. London: Routledge.
Vox-FN. 2006. Du crépuscule a' l'aube, synthèse d'une vision du monde. http://vox-fn.hautetfort.com/archive/2006/02/21/du-crepuscule-a-l-aube-synthese-d-une-vision-du-monde.html. Accessed 5 March 2006.
Weil, Patrick. 1991. *La France et ses Etrangers. L'aventure d'une Politique d'Immigration 1938–1991*. Paris: Calmann-Lévy.
Werts, H., P. Scheepers, and M. Lubbers. 2012. Euro-scepticism and radical right-wing voting in Europe, 2002–2008: Social cleavages, socio-political attitudes and contextual characteristics determining voting for the radical right. *European Union Politics* 14(2): 183–205.
Williams, Michelle H. 2006. *The impact of radical right-wing parties in West European democracies*. New York: Palgrave.
Wolnger, Raymond E., and Steven J. Rosenstone. 1980. *Who Votes?* New Haven: Yale University Press.
Ysmal, Colette. 1991. Les cadres du Front national: les habits neufs de l'extrême droite. In *Sofres: L'état de l'opinion*, eds. Olivier Duhamel and Jérôme Jaffré, 181–197. Paris: Seuil.

Index

A
Activist, 9–11, 15, 16, 20–22, 27, 57–65, 67–77
Age cohort, 88
Anti-establishment, 3, 15, 21, 61
Anti-globalization, 31, 94
Anti-pluralism, 31
Anti-Semitism, 4, 10, 46, 56
Anti-system party, 41, 84, 90, 93, 95
Assimilation, 16, 36, 68
Authoritarianism, 10, 15, 20, 28, 31

B
Bourgeoisie, 83, 96

C
Catch-all, 5, 76, 90, 94, 95
Catholicism, 76
Charismatic leadership, 4, 44, 67, 70
Christianity, 76
Civil society, 71
Clandestine immigrant, 36
Clientelism, 66
Cohabitation, 22, 89
Communitarianism, 34, 36
Communism, 12
Conservativism, 5, 13–15, 17, 44, 45, 66, 81, 83, 84, 96
Crime, 14, 15, 29, 31, 33, 36, 96
Crisis breeds extremism, 89

D
Debt crisis, 34
Delegitimization, 53, 93
Demographics, 59, 68, 76, 80–82, 84, 85, 87

Demonization, 7, 23, 27, 64
Departmental elections, 2, 25, 79, 96
Deportation, 29, 36
Dérapages, 45
Descriptive statistics, 86, 87
Diabolisation, 27, 38–40, 55, 87

E
Economic crisis, 2, 14, 25, 39, 88, 90, 93
Economic nationalism, 19, 35
Economic security, 13
Education, 5, 37, 62, 64, 69, 70, 76, 79, 80, 82, 85–88, 90, 94, 95
Elitism, 4, 31, 32, 35
Ethnicity, 4, 27, 68
European integration, 27, 68, 69, 84, 90, 94
Europeanization, 20, 30, 37, 39, 69, 71
European parliamentary elections, 22, 95
European Union, 3, 20, 31, 32, 34, 36, 60, 69, 71, 76, 84, 94, 97
Extreme right, 5, 7–10, 12, 24, 39, 44, 45, 56, 63, 82

F
Family socialization, 63, 76
Farmer, 83
Far-right, 7–10, 12, 17, 21–23
Fascism, 7
FN ideology, 3, 27, 52, 59, 72, 74, 76, 94–96
FN leadership, 2–4, 18, 25, 26, 40, 43–56
FN membership, 2, 5, 25, 26, 48, 49, 51, 57–77, 90, 93–95, 97
FN voter, 5, 12, 14–18, 23, 25–27, 48, 55, 79, 85, 87, 91, 93–96

Foreigner, 16, 27–30, 33, 36, 67–69, 83, 94
Foreign preference, 36
Formative experience, 63, 64
Framing, 72
French Algeria, 8, 44, 50, 63
French Presidency, 5
Fringe party, 56
Fundamentalism, 17, 36, 84, 89

G
Gender gap, 81, 89

H
Holocaust, 25, 39, 46
Homosexual, 38, 51, 82

I
Identity, 4, 12, 15, 24, 29, 30, 32, 35, 36, 39, 41, 62, 64, 67–69, 72, 73, 80, 93
Ideology, 3, 11–13, 26–41, 44, 47, 48, 52, 53, 56, 57, 59, 61, 63, 64, 66–69, 71–74, 76, 81, 84, 91, 94–96
Illegal immigrant, 14, 28, 33, 36, 94
Immigration, 11, 14–17, 20, 23, 24, 28–41, 45, 65, 68, 69, 71, 80, 82, 83, 90, 94, 97
Inequality, 45
In-group, 36, 72–74
Instrumentality, 34, 40, 55, 72, 97
Interventionism, 11, 19, 45, 52, 68, 96
Iron fist, 4, 44, 47, 51, 56, 96
Islam, 34, 38, 39, 76, 94

L
Laïcité, 33, 34
Leadership crisis, 97
Leadership style, 3, 4, 26, 43–47, 51, 56, 94
Legitimacy, 15, 16, 23, 27
Legitimization, 23
LePenism, 23, 46
Liberalism, 19, 31, 39, 67, 76, 84

M
Manual labour, 14, 65, 83
Marinism, 46
Marital status, 81, 82, 85–87, 89
Media, 3, 4, 12, 13, 16, 18, 19, 23, 24, 38, 43, 52–56, 69, 93, 94

Middle class, 5, 33
Modernization, 5, 27, 40, 76, 79, 82
Multicultural society, 15
Muslim religion, 68, 80

N
Nation, 4, 7, 12, 19, 20, 27, 31, 32, 34–36, 40, 65, 67, 71, 76, 81, 82, 94
National cohesion, 65
National identity, 12, 24, 29, 30, 32, 35, 36, 67
National preference, 19, 29–31, 33, 69, 83, 90
Nationalism, 34, 36, 64
Neoliberalism, 11, 19, 30
Neo-Nazi, 67, 70
Ni droite, ni gauche, 41
Non-voter, 91

O
Open border, 69, 83
Out-group, 36, 72
Outsourcing, 34, 65, 76, 82

P
Parliamentarism, 10
Parliamentary elections, 9, 12, 21–23, 52, 53
Personality cult, 4, 48, 51, 56, 97
Political crisis, 2, 93
Political socialization, 57, 59–67
Political values, 67–71
Populism, 4, 15, 20, 31, 32, 35, 37, 39, 48, 83, 90
Presidential elections, 1, 2, 8, 12, 13, 15, 17, 18, 22–24, 28, 32, 48, 64, 65, 79, 86, 88
Proportional representation, 11, 16
Protectionism, 19
Public insecurity, 27, 29, 40

R
Racism, 12, 36, 61, 67, 70
Radical right, 3, 7, 11, 12, 25, 27, 28, 31, 39–41, 43, 44, 46, 52, 57, 62–65, 67, 72, 76, 80–84, 87, 89, 90, 94
Regional election, 2, 20, 23, 25, 47, 96
Regression, 86, 87
Reindustrialization, 40, 69, 83, 90
Religion, 4, 27, 34, 36, 67, 68, 70, 76, 80
Republicanism, 39
Revisionism, 7, 39, 70

Index

S
Same-sex marriage, 38
Sampling procedure, 28, 47
Satisfaction with democracy, 84, 85, 87
Scapegoat, 29, 83
Second World War, 7, 9, 18, 39, 44–47, 50, 63
Secularism, 40, 46
Self-employed, 83
Self-victimization, 37
Semi-structured interview, 5, 61
Social security, 29, 33, 35
Socialism, 19, 39
Socialization mechanism, 63, 64, 66–67
Sovereignty, 20, 28, 31, 40, 66, 67, 76, 94
Stigmatization, 62, 72, 74–76
Structural opportunity, 94
Supply-and-demand, 3, 93

T
Traditional lifestyle, 82

U
Unemployment, 2, 14–16, 25, 27, 30, 32, 34, 69, 70, 83, 89, 93
Union Pour un Mouvement Populaire (UMPs), 1, 25, 32, 35, 39, 60, 66, 67, 80, 90, 91, 93, 96

V
Victimization discourse, 70
Volksparty, 77

W
Welfare chauvinism, 27, 32, 96
Worker, 4, 5, 21, 24, 32, 35, 39, 40, 82, 83, 85–87, 89, 90, 95

X
Xenophobia, 10, 19, 20, 28, 36

Printed by Printforce, the Netherlands